P9-CAF-417

A complex geometric

A **stepped section** encourages new

Modern building using **indigenous** materials to form campus space

The fenestration is composed to give scale to **human occupancy**

Forms are transformed by a **com**

Sixtee

Extends the **academic fabric** to a new campus boundar

A modular **kit of parts** defines an array of textures that weave through the comple

A **hierarchical organization** stratifies a complex program

wrapped in pre-oxidized copper to announce the entry

The courtyard is a hidden **urban oasis**

ips between teaching and research

Vertical and horizontal **transparencies** filter natural light through the buildin

eclaims space, light, and volume to define a **primordial shelter** for healing

ography, embracing the geometry of the mountains

A bullpen instruction area **redefines** the organic chemistry teaching la

programs are housed in an **academic loft**

Heroic **concrete superstructure** frames ocean and rural view

Elaborate curtain wall and precast wall systems express a **dynamic** building for

The program is organized by a **laminated** array of clusters

THE MASTER ARCHITECT SERIES VI

PAYETTE ASSOCIATES

AN EVOLUTION
OF IDEAS

First published in Australia in 2003
by The Images Publishing Group Pty Ltd
ABN 89 059 734 431
6 Bastow Place, Mulgrave, Victoria, 3170, Australia
Telephone (61 3) 9561 5544 Facsimile (61 3) 9561 4860
Email: books@images.com.au
Website: www.imagespublishinggroup.com

National Library of Australia
Cataloguing-in-Publication data

Payette Associates: selected and current works.
Includes index.
ISBN 1 876907 05 3.
1. Payette Associates. 2. Architects—United States.
I. Crosbie, Mike. II. Title. (Series: Master architect series. VI).

725.0973

Edited by Steve Womersley
Production by The Graphic Image Studio Pty Ltd, Australia
Film by Mission Productions Limited
Printed by Everbest Printing Co. Ltd. in Hong Kong/China

IMAGES has included on its website a page for special notices in
relation to this and our other publications. Please visit this site:
www.imagespublishinggroup.com

CONTENTS

FOREWORD

OBSERVATIONS OF A GRATEFUL CLIENT

Over the past 25 years, I've been the client, more-or-less, for a number of buildings for the Faculty of Arts and Sciences at Harvard. Three of them were new science buildings designed by Payette Associates: for biochemistry, for environmental science, and for computer science. Perhaps I should be more hesitant in singling out one firm from the splendid variety of our architects, who have ranged from those who aimed for an assertive signature to those who were more meekly responsive. Yet I do choose Payette, for they have a characteristic that cannot be fully evident, even from these pages of elegant photographs. Payette Associates bring a deep sensitivity to the principle that structure must serve function.

In biology, structure determines function, whether it's a molecule or an organelle, and that truth inserts itself into every discussion that an architect has with the science professors who will live and work in the building. University faculty aren't known for their quiet acceptance of the creative thoughts of architects, yet Payette Associates have inspired, educated and cajoled, and they have expanded our understanding of how structures can liberate function. They have pushed beyond the design of environments that merely work, to shape places that are inviting, and that foster dialogue and interaction. They have succeeded, too, for their buildings are praised by grateful occupants who teach and do research in spaces filled with light and open views, spaces both for quiet thinking and for collaborative exchange. Persistently and diligently, Payette Associates have convinced us to examine our own creative culture, and they have filled our scientific places with the essence of Harvard's humanist spirit.

These thoughts reflect the delicate guidance and the sensitive concern that Payette Associates have always shown, and suggest how this firm has led a quiet revolution in the design of structures that support the work of the people of science. An enviable record, indeed.

Jeremy R. Knowles, D. Phil.
Dean of the Faculty of Arts and Sciences (1991-2002).
Amory Houghton Professor of Chemistry and Biochemistry, Harvard University.

THE ROAD LESS TRAVELED

Most architects aspire to instant recognition. Starting in architecture school, students venerate those designers whose work can immediately be identified: that building is a Gehry, a Holl, a Hadid. The problem with such fame is that it can lock the architect into a "style prison," the way some movie actors get locked into the characters they portray. The work is bound to become boring, stale, or a caricature of itself. Commissions may flow in because everyone wants a "Bilbao," but the architect becomes tethered to a market image. An alternative is to approach each design problem with an inquisitive nature, liberated from formalistic convention, and respond as the local conditions suggest. One thinks of an architect such as Eero Saarinen, who explored each problem from a fresh, new perspective. In architecture, this is the road less traveled.

The architects of Payette Associates travel this road. Evidence abounds in this volume, which cogently presents the history of the firm, its dedication to both the science and spirit of architecture, the lasting values that can be found throughout its work, and themes that can make architecture timeless. Few architects are articulate about their own work. Payette Associates is an exception. They have thought deeply about the principles inherent in their architecture, and present them here as an evolution of ideas.

Founded in the 1930s, the first generation of Payette's practice was built on a bedrock of observation, problem solving, and responsible design. Its second generation of architects, starting in the 1960s, pursued an "indigenous modernism," best found in a series of hospitals constructed in New England. In their design was all of the intelligent planning that marked the first generation, combined with an eye for local color—in this case an architecture that embodied an enduring Yankee severity. At the Aga Kahn University in Pakistan, where Payette's work includes master planning and a hospital, medical college, and nursing school, Payette's acuity to cultural context blossomed like a flower in the desert. Careful study of the vernacular architecture in this part of the world yielded a creation that is true to its place and time.

The last few years have seen major changes at Payette, with a third generation now at the helm. The evidence in this monograph indicates that these architects continue to build upon the firm's architectural principles. Ongoing work at such institutions as Harvard, Princeton, Brown, Oberlin, and others, focuses on the creation of campus communities, not just individual buildings. At Carnegie Mellon University, a new laboratory building complements a major landmark, while at Yale a diminutive structure expresses the power possible in carefully detailed materials. In a Providence, Rhode Island neighborhood, an addition to an existing hospital introduces a new formal language that nonetheless is sympathetic to nearby residential and industrial buildings.

Payette's arc of design over the past 70 years could not have been planned. But the continuity is there, and for Payette that has made all the difference.

Michael J. Crosbie, Ph.D.
Dr. Crosbie is an architect, teacher, journalist, and
critic whose work has been published internationally.

FIRM HISTORY AND VALUES

FIRM HISTORY

VALUES
MOVEMENT
LIGHT / SHADOW
INSIDE / OUTSIDE
RITUAL AND CEREMONY
COLOR

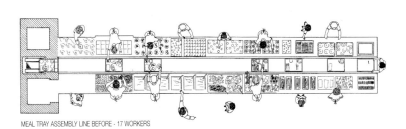

MEAL TRAY ASSEMBLY LINE BEFORE - 17 WORKERS

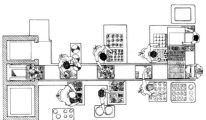

AFTER - 8 WORKERS

Time-and-Motion Study, Pittsfield General Hospital,1958 - Food services and other processes were studied to optimize space and staffing needs

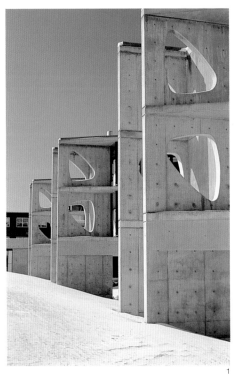

The Jordan Hospital, 1976 - An early example of the firm's modernist approach to New England Hospitals

The roots of Payette Associates extend to 1932, when architect Paul Nocka and Frederick Markus, an engineer and industrial designer, worked together on the landmark New York Hospital. They left Shepley Rutan and Coolidge in Boston to form Markus and Nocka Architects and Engineers. With a mixture of scientific management and planning efficiency, Markus and Nocka focused on small experimental and prototype hospital projects. From the human ballet choreographed in their own time-and-motion studies, the two conceived of new geometric hospital configurations that emphasized productivity and labor-savings. Markus and Nocka carefully considered every functional part of the contemporary hospital for the next 30 years.

Tom Payette joined Markus and Nocka after graduating from the Harvard Graduate School of Design in 1960, becoming a partner in 1965. John Wilson and Dave Rowan joined the firm in 1966 to work on Leonard Morse Hospital, forming the foundation of what would become Payette Associates in 1974, after Markus and Nocka retired. The firm enlarged its client base to include colleges and universities, schools of medicine, and corporations as well as hospitals.

In 1998, Payette Associates completed a successful transition of leadership and ownership when James H. Collins Jr. was elected president and the principals of the firm took on more equal participation.

These changes in leadership have brought new energy and focus to the firm.

Today the firm is comprised of approximately 120 people and has a global practice. Organized as three highly collaborative design studios, at the firm's core are the same issues that so preoccupied Markus and Nocka more than 70 years ago. We are still fascinated with architecture that serves highly technical programs. We are humanists at our core, and we take seriously our responsibility in the design of spaces in which some of life's most significant experiences and discoveries will occur.

FIRM HISTORY

The foundation of our practice is based upon problem solving. We strive for innovation by understanding the subtle nuances of a client's site, program needs, and technological aspirations.

Principals: (Back Row) Robert F. Mattox, Thomas M. Payette, John L. Wilson, (Front Row) Jonathan B. Romig, George E. Marsh, Jr., James H. Collins, Jr., Sho-Ping Chin, J. Ian Adamson, Kevin B. Sullivan, Robert J. Schaeffner, Jr., Jeffery J. Burke

Design pin-ups, a forum for office-wide discussion where the design studios share ideas on a bi-weekly basis, are an integral part of the firm's culture

On average, Payette's 11 principals have been with the firm for over 20 years. Our wealth of experience with technically demanding building typologies has resulted in more than 80 design awards. We have been fortunate to collaborate with some of the best minds at some of the most forward-thinking medical and academic institutions in the world, which has allowed our practice to thrive. Today, the firm's values remain focused on people and on designing authentic, sophisticated, and complex environments.

Our firm has a very optimistic view of the architect's power to make a positive impact upon their own communities and the world at large, shaping spaces and lives in dramatic new ways. This view extends beyond our own work into the realm of social action, such as providing solutions for housing for the homeless, which we have organized for over a decade.

We believe in modernity and an architecture of permanence and craft, inspired by its place to reinterpret form and culture. Because of this belief, our architecture is undeniably eclectic. Each project is distinctive, with its own set of discoveries and innovations. Yet, we remain extremely practical, tied to our roots, as we develop new prototypes for our clients. We design buildings that promote human interaction, provide comfort and solace, and support the exchange of ideas.

MOVEMENT

Architecture is a kinesthetic art. You move through it not with your eyes but with your entire body and being. Stairways, corridors, bridges, and elevators are the street life of buildings.

1

2

3

4

5

6

1

LIGHT / SHADOW

*It is vital to bring natural light into the
heart of a building, to always sense
where the outside is. The pattern of
light complements the daily rhythms
of the life inside. Solid and transparent
walls create the boundaries between
privacy and community.*

3

5

4

The building and its site are one com-

position of solid and void. Each forms

the other, an inhabited unity.

4

5

RITUAL AND CEREMONY

Architecture starts with envisioning

the particular rituals and ceremonies

to be performed in a building, then

brings them to light and life.

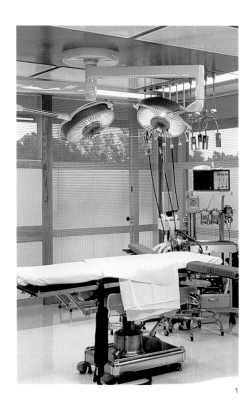

1

2

4

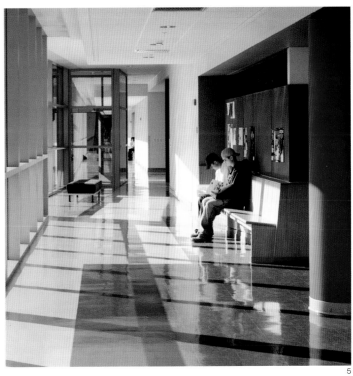

5

1

2

COLOR

The colors of earth, sea, and sky are

different around the world. There is

even palpability to the light and air in

every place. Each building needs its

own palette of color that comes from

its inner life and place in the world.

4

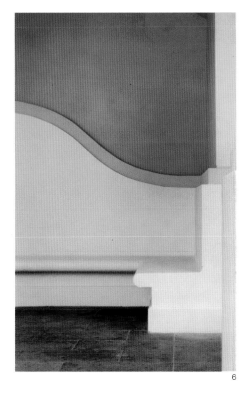

6

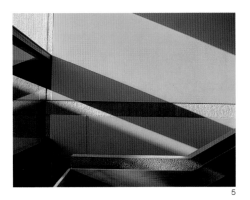

5

PROJECTS

The heart of our design practice is the creation of settings for lives spent in intensive interaction with some of the most sophisticated technology modern society has produced. Our architecture supports people, individually and collectively, in pursuing those lives to their fullest.

This book can be read on several levels and is designed to reveal the many connections of theme, project type, and value as they blend to enrich the firm's architecture, reflecting an evolution of ideas.Throughout this book, our ideas are clustered in three strands: "The Art and Science of Building," "Social Geometry," and "Site Context."

There are multiple layers in each project's presentation. The first layer—the photographs—reflects the physical nature and aesthetic appeal of the architecture. The second layer—plans, sections, elevations, diagrams, and other drawings—reveals the rigor of each project's design. The third layer—the strands of text mentioned above—weaves the themes of our work throughout the projects, while the fourth layer—the project descriptions—provides a narrative recounting the project's history, design approach, and significance within Payette's body of work.

? How can this language also provide identity and understanding of the building's inner order how it comes toge

The Art and Science of Building

What is the right language of form, materials, and building assembly to express the inner life of the architecture in its place, culture, and climate? How can this language also provide identity and understanding of the building's inner order—how it comes together, and how it can be used?

What is the purpose or use of the building, and how do its program and parti shape it? How are these activities interrelated and supported three-dimensionally? What is the life of the building, inside and out, day and night, through time?

Social Geometry

ted three-dimensionally? What is the life of the building, inside and out, day and night, through time? What pur

How does the building relate to the past, present, and future of its surroundings? How does architecture restore, repair, and create patterns of space and circulation that transform its setting?

Site Context

eate patterns of space and circulation that transform its setting how the building relate to the past,

NEW ENGLAND ROOTS

1

Leonard Morse Hospital in Natick, Massachusetts, and the five healthcare projects presented with it were some of the first projects completed by our firm. They set a tone of architectural invention in the context of our New England practice, which sought to infuse contemporary design with a regional character. (We might call it "Yankee Modernism.") The work is distinguished by a simple, spare material palette of exposed concrete, mahogany, and glass. The use of the concrete frame allows for flexible interior layouts and the ability to expand the building either horizontally or vertically. These six projects also reflect a new sensibility in hospital design, one centered on the experience of the patient.

LEONARD MORSE HOSPITAL

Leonard Morse Hospital's goals are to better serve a growing population and to accommodate the skills of local doctors, many of whom also practice at nearby Boston teaching hospitals. We were retained for master planning and a major renovation and addition to the hospital.

The hospital's New England site is heavily wooded, with irregular terrain and an exposed ledge. It made economic and aesthetic sense to use the more level parts of the site for parking and to fit the multilevel hospital addition into the ledge, with a link to other functions in the converted existing buildings.

1 MAIN ENTRY
2 ER ENTRY
3 PATIENT TOWER
4 ICU
5 SURGERY
6 X-RAY

0   64   128ft

Bold modern forms **frame** the natural landscape.

Leonard Morse - Patient Unit

The form is the result of the **clustering** of patient rooms.

MARY LANE HOSPITAL

Located in the small town of Ware, Massachusetts, the scope of services included master planning, programming, design, and construction of 120,000 square feet of hospital facilities and medical offices. The exterior textured walls provide a contrast to the surrounding trees, whose thin shadows stretch across the gray concrete canvas.

ANNA JACQUES HOSPITAL

Anna Jacques is a privately owned general hospital serving Newburyport, Massachusetts and the surrounding suburban communities on Boston's North Shore. Its architecture is a variation on the theme of Leonard Morse. The plan reflects the modular quality of the concrete frame construction, clearly expressing the individual patient rooms, which are grouped in pods of four. This arrangement is immediately apparent on the exterior, with its exposed concrete walls, large windows (which deliver ample light to patient areas), and exposed mahogany infill panels that have weathered to a silvery hue to complement the concrete.

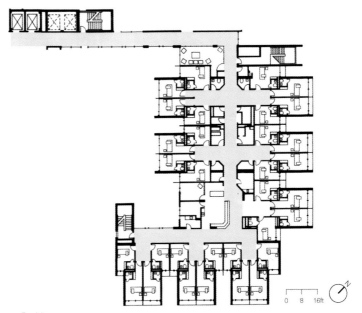

Anna Jacques - Level 1

ANDROSCOGGIN VALLEY HOSPITAL

Built as a complete replacement for an obsolete hospital in New Hampshire, this new facility is located on 38 acres along the Androscoggin River. The wish to preserve existing trees, surface land features, and underground ledge contours strongly influenced the placement of the hospital on the site and its spatial organization. As do the hospitals following Leonard Morse, the building has a poured-in-place, reinforced concrete frame.

6

EASTERN MAINE MEDICAL CENTER

A 275,000-square-foot addition with a tower orientated to give all the new patient rooms dramatic views stands at the core of the master plan. This project shows a further refinement of the concrete frame approach, with a bolder exploration of its volumetric possibilities. The architecture also reflects the influence of Jose Luis Sert, who was a design studio critic for several of the firm's partners when they studied at Harvard. The building surmounts its sloped site and opens itself to views of the nearby Penobscot River, and also to generous sunlight for the patient rooms. Formally there is an expression of individual rooms, clusters of rooms, and wings.

7

EMERSON HOSPITAL

Emerson Hospital has grown from a country hospital to a suburban medical center under the design guidance of our firm since 1961. Several additions and new construction projects use extensive floor-to-ceiling glass and a reinforced concrete structure to maximize the exposure of interior spaces to natural light and a lushly wooded site. Noteworthy is the plan's use of a large, glassy perimeter corridor that rings clusters of intensive care units. Staff and family areas are separate, allowing for a greater measure of privacy and a less stressful environment.

9

10

8

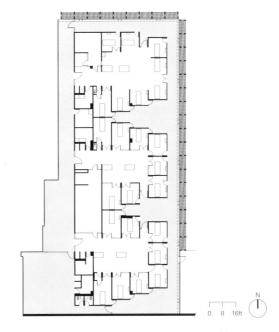

Emerson Hospital - ICU pod with perimeter corridor

0 8 16ft

N

JORDAN HOSPITAL

Plymouth, Massachusetts

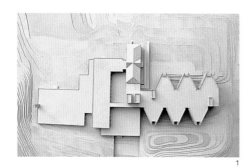

1

Jordan Hospital sits amid historic Plymouth, site of the first permanent European settlement in New England, and now a fishing and tourist center with ship-related industries and cranberry-packing houses. The new hospital addition with its expressive concrete superstructure gives Jordan Hospital a commanding presence, shifting the building's center of gravity to the new main entrance. The addition is carefully sited across a rolling hill, its saw-toothed layout containing patient rooms with views toward Plymouth Bay.

The building's inner life is expressed on the facades, and the structure derives from its configuration. Projecting concrete overhangs and vertical fins provide summer shading for this south-facing addition. Wards are raised on concrete piers, freeing the area beneath for vehicular circulation and the major public entry.

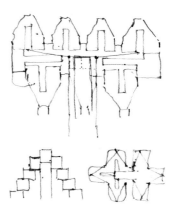

2

A heroic **concrete superstructure** frames ocean and rural views.

34

3

4

5

6

1   ORIGINAL 1924 BUILDING
2   8-BED NURSING UNIT
3   SUPPORT CORE
4   DIAGNOSTIC SERVICE

0   16   32ft

Level 2

Shifting symmetry and **program geometry** bring natural light to the core of the building

7

8

A floor of 48 single-bed rooms is organized in eight-bed clusters. Shifting the symmetry by offsetting the clusters brings natural light to the core of the floor. Cluster variations were developed for intensive and coronary care, pediatrics, and mental health.

supported three-dimensionally? What

JOSLIN DIABETES FOUNDATION I MEDICAL RESEARCH FACILITY
Boston, Massachusetts

1

The Joslin Diabetes Foundation is dedicated to improving the lives of people with diabetes and its complications through innovative care, education, and research that will lead to prevention and cure of the disease. The planning objective of this project was to meet immediate and long-term needs. Designed and constructed to accommodate three additional floors in the future without interruption to daily operations, the building integrates healthcare and research within a tight urban site.

2

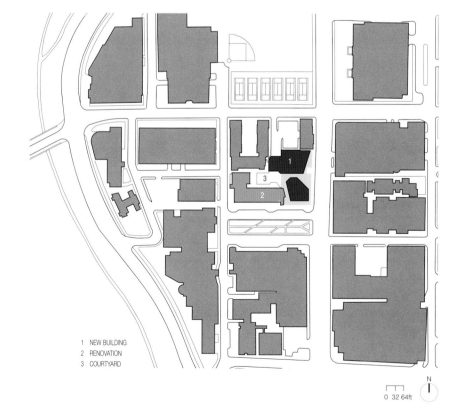

1 NEW BUILDING
2 RENOVATION
3 COURTYARD

0 32 64ft

N

The courtyard is a hidden **urban oasis**.

38

The facility, which houses both inpatient and outpatient components, contains a central courtyard—green space shared by two existing Joslin facilities. This outdoor green space allows natural light to permeate an existing building where patients reside and promotes the interaction of staff and patients. This landscape area also serves as a healing space, where patients and families can enjoy an outside environment protected from the surrounding urban context. The main circulation from a parking garage flows along the perimeter of the space and along the edges of the building's main lobby.

Within 144,600 square feet of new space and 14,000 square feet of renovation, there are 71 beds for diabetes treatment and research, with a full complement of inpatient services. There are also outpatient and clinical areas, laboratories for endocrinology, microbiology, neuroscience, dermatology, and animal research. The clustering of 20 exam rooms around a central nursing station permits an efficient flow of patients and doctors. The ground floor houses commercial space that supports the patients and families of those who stay at the facility. This building and the foundation's way of supporting research and caring for people with diabetes has become a model around the world.

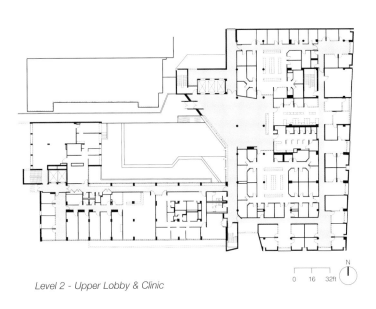

Level 2 - Upper Lobby & Clinic

0   16   32ft

N

4

5

6

HOULTON REGIONAL HOSPITAL

Houlton, Maine

1

This new hospital, sited in a potato field in Maine's Aroostook County, is the culmination of a long effort to merge the strengths of two small hospitals in the town into one large healthcare institution.

A major design determinant was the harsh winter climate. Temperatures often dip to as low as -40°F for days. For protection, the building was conceived as an "inside-out refrigerator," with insulation wrapping it like a parka. The "light-house" floor's high color bands visually tie the building wings together and make a striking counterpoint to the rolling fields of green or blankets of snow.

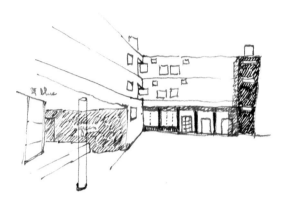

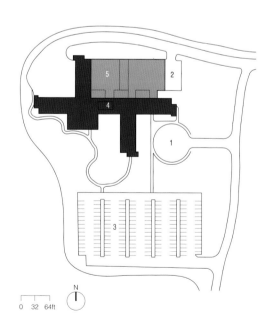

1   MAIN ENTRY
2   ER DROP OFF
3   PARKING
4   INPATIENT WING
5   DIAGNOSTIC & TREATMENT

N

0   32   64ft

the building **Color and pattern** register a building surrounded by potato fields and snow.

2

3

Multiple spaces are not commodities to be identified only by number. Bright colors are used to identify patient wings and distinct spaces such as dressing rooms, elevator cabs, elevator lobbies, and operating rooms, while also aiding in way-finding. Views to the exterior and natural light (both direct and reflected) are the focus of every patient area. The inverted mirror image allows long views from a floor of 72 single beds, comprised of two 36-bed units with 18-bed sub-units. Small windows are carefully placed to light walls and ceilings and to provide views for people standing, sitting, or lying down. While the summer sun can drive the temperature into the high 90s, operable windows allow ample breezes, while sunset brings radiational cooling.

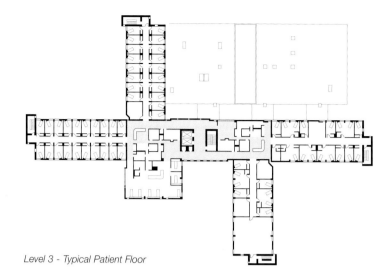

Level 3 - Typical Patient Floor

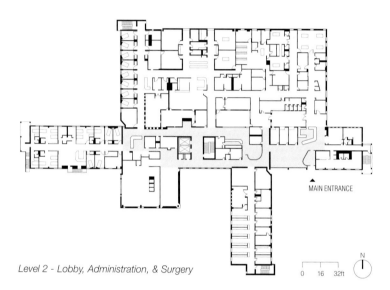

Level 2 - Lobby, Administration, & Surgery

MAIN ENTRANCE

N

0   16   32ft

A **hub & spoke** plan defines a new regional hospital.

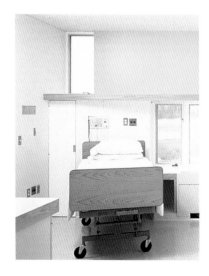
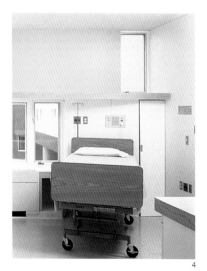

4

5

is the life of the building, inside and out, day and night, through time? What

6

7

HARVARD UNIVERSITY
SHERMAN FAIRCHILD BIOCHEMISTRY LABORATORY

Cambridge, Massachusetts

1

Harvard University sought a contemporary
building that would respect the materials
and character of the context, while providing state-of-the-art facilities and safe-
guards for biochemistry researchers and
the surrounding community. A library and
other functions were to be shared in an
adjacent building. This project was our
first academic research facility, and
reflects themes of community and transparency used in later laboratory projects.

The new building transforms the existing
residential context (which was sprinkled
with parking lots) to one more appropriate
for academic life, complete with landscaped quadrangles and pedestrian
paths that enrich and extend the pattern of
historic Harvard Yard. The new 105,000-
square-foot building joins to the older
Gibbs building directly west of it, creating
a new courtyard. While Gibbs serves as
the focal point of this protected oasis, the
two sides of Fairchild facing the courtyard
are transparent, allowing views into the
labs and other spaces. In contrast, the
new building faces out to the street with
heavy brick walls punched with rectangular openings, echoing the materials,
massing, and fenestration of the older
structures nearby.

1 SHERMAN FAIRCHILD
   BIOCHEMISTRY LABORATORY
2 RENOVATED CHEMISTRY
3 COURTYARD

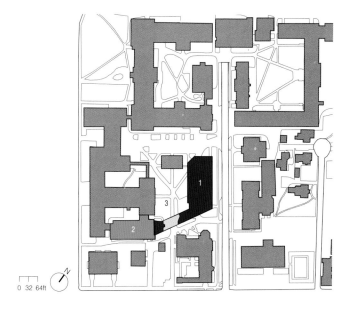

0 32 64ft

A modern university building using **indigenous** materials to form campus space.

46

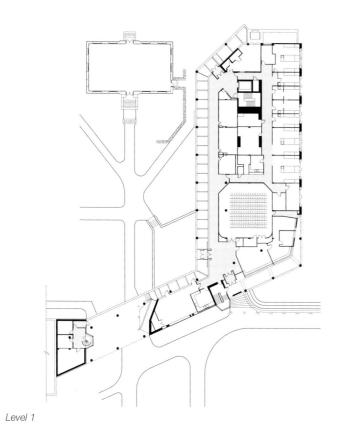

Level 1

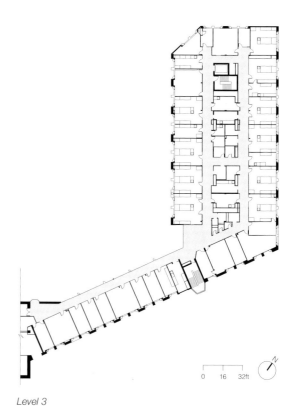

Level 3

0   16   32ft

Visual **transparency** transforms a laboratory environment for the first time

Wherever possible, glass interior walls are used to allow each lab to function as a separately controlled environment while also encouraging awareness of fellow researchers in neighboring lab spaces. Shared instrument rooms open vistas within. Such a design helps to foster a community of researchers.

2

3

...nd out, day and night, through time? Wh...

4

REACHING OUT

THE AGA KHAN UNIVERSITY
HOSPITAL, MEDICAL COLLEGE, SCHOOL OF NURSING

Karachi, Pakistan

1

On the western edge of the Indus delta near the Kirthar mountain range lies Karachi, a modern desert city by the sea. Like so many cities in the developing world, Karachi is being transformed by modern technology, which results in more jobs, much-needed housing, and higher educational standards. With the advent of industrialization and mass-production, members of the worldwide Muslim community are increasingly finding themselves alienated in a physical environment that no longer expresses deeply rooted traditions and cultural values.

A major force in the heart of the developing world, the Aga Khan University represents both a link to the great Islamic academic traditions of the past and a bold, progressive action aimed at providing education and healthcare services to people in Pakistan and South Asia.

1 GATE HOUSE
2 MOSQUE
3 FILTER CLINIC
4 MEDICAL COLLEGE
5 MALE DORMITORIES
6 PRIVATE PATIENT WING
7 HOSPITAL
8 NURSING SCHOOL AND
   FEMALE DORMITORIES
9 SERVICE BUILDING

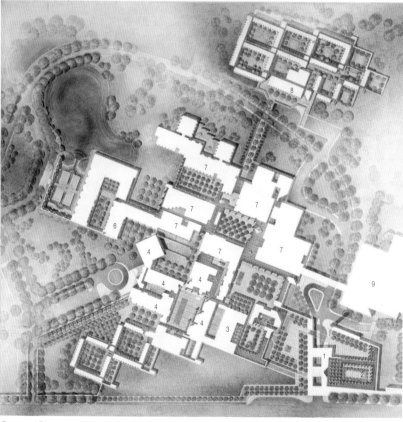

Campus Plan - 1985

A modern academic/medical **campus** has emerged as an oasis in the desert.

52

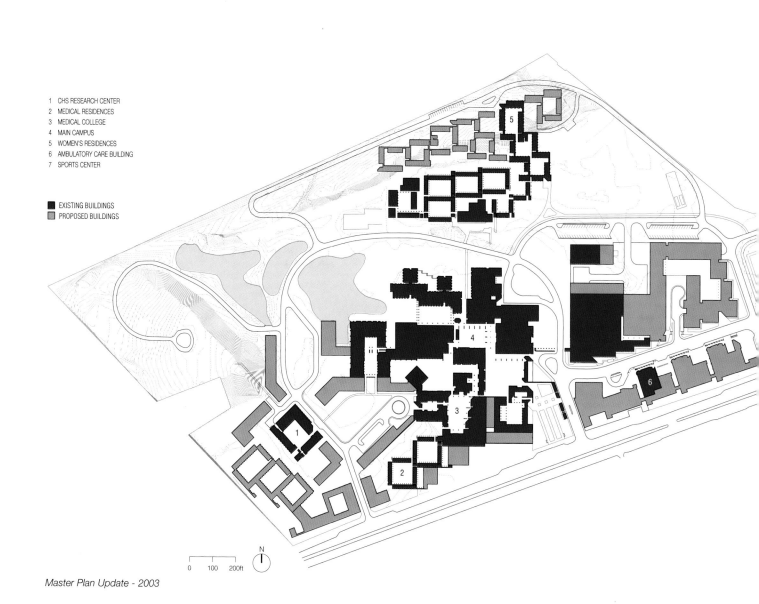

1 CHS RESEARCH CENTER
2 MEDICAL RESIDENCES
3 MEDICAL COLLEGE
4 MAIN CAMPUS
5 WOMEN'S RESIDENCES
6 AMBULATORY CARE BUILDING
7 SPORTS CENTER

■ EXISTING BUILDINGS
■ PROPOSED BUILDINGS

0   100   200ft

N

Master Plan Update - 2003

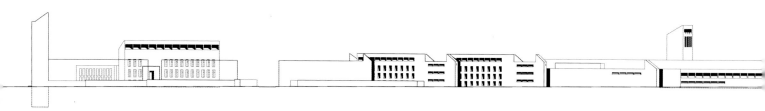

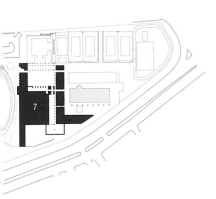

7

Located on 64 acres donated by the Government of Pakistan, the Aga Khan University was conceived in 1970 as the cornerstone of a philanthropic commitment to address a shortage of trained medical personnel and to improve healthcare delivery throughout Pakistan. His Highness Prince Karim Aga Khan, leader of the world's Ismaili Muslims, worked closely with us to develop comprehensive planning and design guidelines to ensure that the new complex would incorporate state-of-the-art educational and medical technology, while demonstrating that a modern architectural solution could preserve the spirit of the culture, rather than superficially mimic its forms.

The Aga Khan Hospital, Medical College, and School of Nursing were granted university status by the President of Pakistan in 1981. In addition to the 721-bed teaching hospital, the original campus, completed in 1985, included a Filter Clinic (providing free medical care to the poorest of Karachi's residents); a Medical School (training physicians to work at the community level in rural areas as well as in urban institutional settings); and a School of Nursing. Separate housing facilities are provided for male and female students, as well as administrative offices, support services, and physical plant facilities.

Entry Portal, Great Mosque of Cordoba, Spain (ca. 784-786)

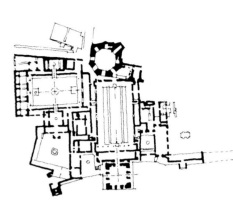

Plan, The Alhambra, Granada, Spain (Mid 13th C. - Late 14th C.)

At the project's start, the design team undertook an on-site study of historic Islamic architecture in Spain, North Africa, Iran, and Pakistan, conducted with reference to the cultural background of each area. Special attention was paid to the specific architectural expression that is the outcome of an indigenous way of life. The team was convinced that, aside from learning about the impact geography and climate had on these precedents, its members should become intimately familiar with the history and social trends of the area—underlying forces that help shape architecture.

The team researched the history of Islamic hospitals, learning that the earliest hospital was built in Syria by Caliph al-Wahid in 707. Eighty years later, the Caliph of Baghdad Haroun al-Rashid attached a college (madrasa) to every mosque and a hospital to every college. From its earliest inception, the college, hospital, and mosque were linked. Teaching and the advancement of medicine were seen as integral parts of a hospital's function.

1	MALE HOSTELS	11	DOCTORS LOUNGE
2	LAB	12	TRANSCRIPTION
3	COMMUNITY CLINIC	13	PATIENT ROOMS
4	LECTURE HALL	14	PATIENT WARDS
5	PROFESSORS OFFICES	15	X-RAY
6	LIBRARY	16	EMERGENCY
7	AUDITORIUM	17	OUTPATIENT
8	ADMINISTRATION	18	GATE HOUSE
9	PHYSICAL THERAPY	19	LOCKER ROOMS
10	ENTRY LOBBY	20	PLANT
		21	WATER STORAGE

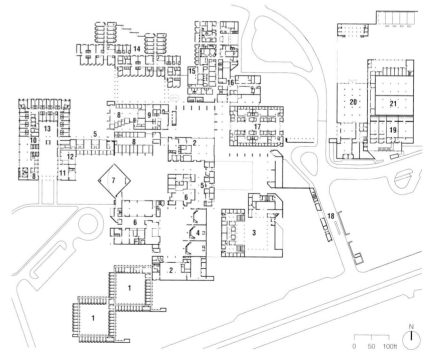

Ground Floor Plan - Core Campus

The planning is a **synthesis** of modern city planning and traditional Islamic architectural values.

56

By the 12th century, hospitals were in use throughout the Islamic world and made their way to Europe by way of the Crusaders, who marveled at these "new" institutions.

In addition, the team studied significant Islamic architectural precedents, such as the Alhambra Palace complex in Granada, the Qarauin Mosque in Fez, the Mausoleum of Sultan Hassan in Cairo, the Masjed-I-Shah and Meydan-I-Shah complexes in Isfahan, and Akbar Fort and Shalimar Gardens in Lahore. Based on this research, a multi-layered set of guidelines was established for the physical layout, architectural development, landscape, and interior design of the facility, based on local culture, climate, and the specific attributes of the site.

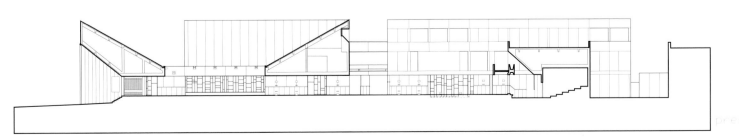

DESIGN PRINCIPLES

Identification of Parts

The diverse physical requirements of the individual components are incorporated into a single organic whole, while the different architectural functions are represented through the identification of appropriate entrances, portals, changes of level, vistas, reflecting pools, and landscape elements.

The Exterior Room

The design places a higher value on the interconnectedness of spaces than on buildings-as-objects. Space and function are based on the courtyard, outdoor rooms for gathering and social interaction, surrounded by the enclosed program spaces inside the building complex. Here, architecture is a continuous progression of "interiorized" outdoor spaces that surround the observer, rather than "object buildings" that stand apart and are aloof.

Sequence of Spaces

The procession of spaces is not simply a series of similar courtyards designed for aesthetic reasons alone, but rather a sequence of interlocking exterior spaces that vary in function, scale, and proportion. Some

The most **advanced healthcare** planning and delivery systems in the developing world.

courtyards are designed for private contemplation. Others define waiting areas for patients' family members and visitors, while those in the medical school and school of nursing encourage student interaction. The design of each courtyard is carefully calibrated to the specific patterns of use that occur in and around them.

Threshold Between Courtyards

The manner of transition between courtyards is significant. These thresholds are sensitively handled, signaling changes in function and preparing the observer for the succeeding architectural experiences. Each transition space partially or completely conceals the full impact of the courtyard yet to be entered.

ed three-dimensionally? What is t

8

9

10

11

Movement Through Architecture

As the courtyards unfold in a rhythmic and hierarchical sequence, one acquires a profound experience that cannot be attributed to any singular architectural episode or to any specified point in time. The experience is derived from the integrated whole of the complex while observed and experienced in a state of motion.

Indigenous Building Technology

All of the significant traditional architectural works in Islamic cultures demonstrate a high level of collaboration among architects, builders, and indigenous artists and craftsmen. The rich elaborations of tile designers, muqarnas workers, ornamental metal artisans, calligraphers, mill workers, plasterers, marble engravers, and textile weavers cannot be separated from the aesthetic of the whole. The University makes extensive use of indigenous materials, processes, and systems. Moreover, the design provided the opportunity for this project to serve as a catalyst to advance the building technology and materials industry within Pakistan.

Arrival and Entry

Entrance portals are given special attention in historic Islamic buildings. Often they are the only means by which an architectural function is identified. They also signify the beginning of a new architectural and esthetic experience. Here, monumental portals are used to identify points of entry to the major divisions of the University (Hospital, Medical College, and School of Nursing). The importance of these entry points is underscored by carefully lining these portals in a pink marble quarried in the mountains of northern Pakistan. In many cases the marble is inscribed with Koranic verses in Kufic script.

Architecture for the Senses

The design of the interior and exterior surfaces responds to the different human senses as well as the need for meditation, interaction, privacy, and motion. The reinforced concrete and concrete block buildings are rendered in "weeping plaster," a naturally pigmented cement plaster with a hue that is easy on the eye in the intense sun and which reduces glare by casting its own shadow. Marble wainscoting is used where people come into contact with exterior walls. Weeping plaster and terra cotta and teak screens (sight), running water (sound), flower beds (smell), and marble and teak (touch) form an architecture of the senses that supports and enhances the spatial experience.

Response to Local Climate

The design flows from a site-specific strategy that embraces climate as a fundamental constraint. By deploying traditional techniques of passive climate control—terra cotta brise soleil, sloped roofs with wind scoops, courtyard design, use of water, and wall mass—dependence upon air-conditioning was reduced in a region where electrical service is not dependable. The resulting building forms work with nature and provide a link with tradition.

12

13

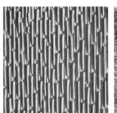

14–17

GROWTH, CHANGE, AND THE FUTURE

The initial campus, completed in 1985, provided approximately one million square feet of space for hospital, academic, and housing functions. This original commission has evolved into a prolific, ongoing relationship between the University and our firm that now spans more than three decades. In the 1990s, we were commissioned to prepare a master plan to identify sites for new and expanding programs and to integrate newly acquired land into a comprehensive plan for growth. Following this master plan, the firm designed an expansion of teaching facilities for the School of Nursing (1995) and an addition to the radiology department, which included a new MRI unit (1996).

Shortly thereafter, the new Community Health Services and Research Buildings and the Sports and Rehabilitation Center were completed, the first of what is anticipated to be a series of new buildings that will create a new medical research campus to the west of the main hospital.

In 1999, our firm was commissioned to revise and update the master plan to respond to pressing space constraints stemming from newly emerging areas of growth. The new master plan for a series of building and renovation projects over the next decade includes an Ambulatory Care Building, a Cardiac Services Building, an expansion to the existing surgical suite, the Women's Residences complex, an Oncology Building, a Clinical Laboratory, and expansions to the physical plant.

Beyond the specific programs already identified by the University, the master plan identifies the potential for new patterns of development to emerge. The master plan will remain a work in progress, a living document that will continue to evolve over time to meet the changing needs of the University, while preserving the essential values and qualities embedded in the design of the original campus.

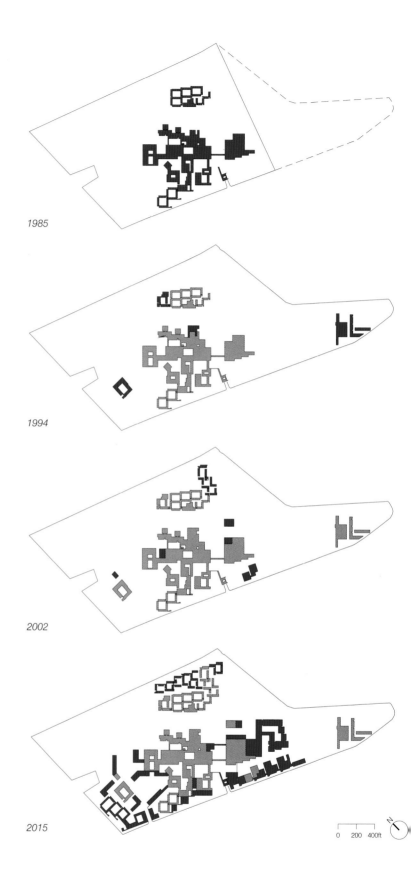

1985

1994

2002

2015

0   200   400ft

PRINCETON UNIVERSITY CAMPUS PLANNING

Princeton, New Jersey

1

Princeton University has a unique and distinctive campus environment. Modeled after Oxford University in England, the campus plan includes a spacious green surrounded by cloistered quadrangles of buildings.

Our firm's relationship with Princeton University began in 1982, with a significant addition/renovation to the Frick/Hoyt chemistry complex. Shortly thereafter the firm began the design of the Lewis Thomas Laboratory—the first molecular biology facility on a college campus—which was completed in 1984. This new building was a refreshing alternative to the notion of conducting modern scientific inquiry in obsolete, outdated laboratory buildings.

The planning and construction of the buildings at Princeton have always included a careful consideration of the relationship of the building to the campus walks. This connection is an essential part of the experience of Princeton's campus. The institution, however, never turned its back on the Gothic tradition. We have been able to express a more contemporary version of the style while at the same time accommodating the growth of the campus.

does the building relate to the past, present, and future of its surroundings? How does our architecture have **Key modern structures** have

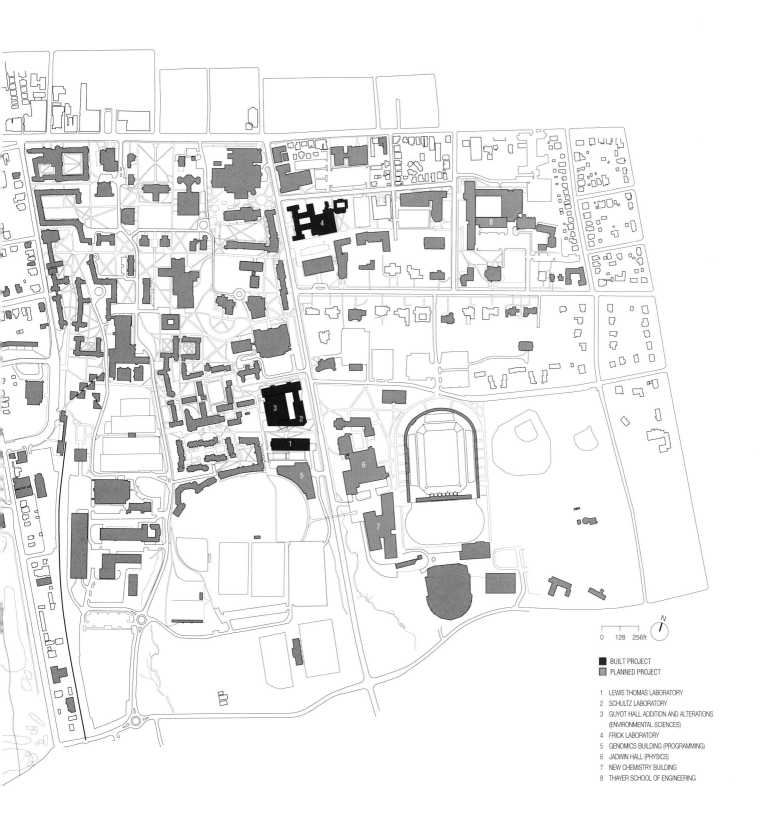

BUILT PROJECT
PLANNED PROJECT

1 LEWIS THOMAS LABORATORY
2 SCHULTZ LABORATORY
3 GUYOT HALL ADDITION AND ALTERATIONS
   (ENVIRONMENTAL SCIENCES)
4 FRICK LABORATORY
5 GENOMICS BUILDING (PROGRAMMING)
6 JADWIN HALL (PHYSICS)
7 NEW CHEMISTRY BUILDING
8 THAYER SCHOOL OF ENGINEERING

0   128   256ft

N

tely inserted on the quintessential Collegiate Gothic campus.

PRINCETON UNIVERSITY I LEWIS THOMAS LABORATORY
Princeton, New Jersey

The Lewis Thomas Molecular Biology Laboratory is well suited to the Princeton University campus. The building integrates and balances state-of-the-art technology with behavioral and contextual issues. It contains research labs, administrative offices, teaching labs, building support areas, lecture halls, and storage space. One of the aims of the University in creating this new facility was to consolidate various branches of the biological sciences located throughout the campus. This consolidation required an integration of space that promotes personal interaction while still providing labs flexible enough for different kinds of research. The result was the first open academic laboratory, complete with exposed building systems.

The building creates an entrance to the main campus on Goheen Walk, reinforcing the walk's importance. As a simple rectangular form, the lab reflects the loft-like, repetitive program spaces inside.

The exterior's brick with stone trim (the result of a collaborative design with Venturi, Scott Brown and Associates) relates to the typical building materials in this part of the campus. Surface pattern and fine detailing provide the large, flat facade with richness and scale reminiscent of the three-dimensional facades of older buildings nearby.

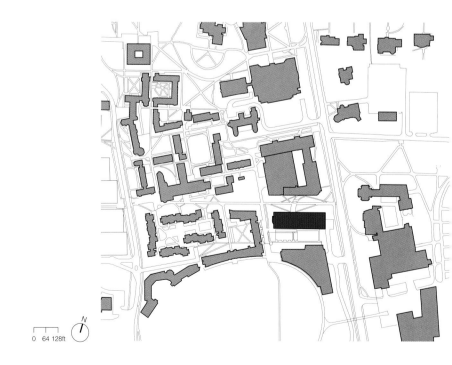

0   64 128ft
N

The science environment is **integrated** into a traditional university culture.

THE WIESS-ELKINS TEACHING CENTER

2

3

create patterns of space and circulation that transform its setting?   he past

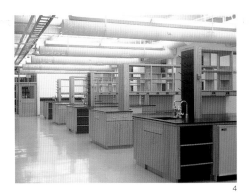

4

In order to provide the best possible conditions for the researchers, all laboratory space is located at the building's periphery, with generous natural light. Equipment is stored at the building's center. Windows between labs and internal support spaces deliver light and views throughout the building's width. Such visual connections promote awareness of fellow researchers in a building containing numerous separately controlled environments. Teaching and research labs share support spaces and circulation paths, encouraging interaction among the faculty and students.

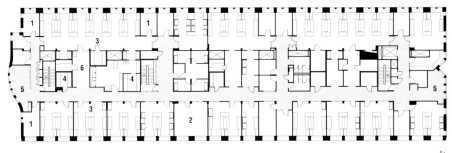

1 OFFICE
2 CONFERENCE
3 LAB
4 SPECIAL LAB
5 LOUNGE/BREAK AREA
6 SUPPORT

0 8 16ft

N

5

6

7

With the pressing need for highly adaptable labs, a four-person research module with adjacent mechanical shafts was introduced for all laboratories. The modules easily accommodate additional services and partitions as needed; for example, an instrument space can be transformed into a biochemistry lab, or a seminar room into a physics lab.

Not only are the wainscoting, doors, door frames, furniture, and laboratory casework solid and durable but the material also adds warmth to this state-of-the-art laboratory setting.

ATHENS REGIONAL MEDICAL CENTER

Athens, Georgia

1

The development of a master plan for Athens Regional Medical Center takes the form of a family of projects. These projects restore the hospital's main entrance to historic Prince Avenue (the old Atlanta Highway) and integrate it with the Athens neighborhood.

A new tower addition to the north wing includes a 24-bed ICU complex above an LDR/intensive care nursery. Other spaces include a Physical Therapy/Occupational Therapy department, a ground floor coffee/ gift shop, and a new linear accelerator suite. A new Substance Abuse Treatment Center (SATC) is located in a renovated brick veneer garden apartment building south of the hospital, which once housed nurses and interns. The new center contains space for recreation, dining, meeting, counseling, administration, new fireproof sleeping units, and a detox unit.

The east end of the hospital now includes a new emergency department with separate entrances for ambulances, walk-ins, and outpatients. Adjacent existing spaces were remodeled for imaging, endoscopy, and cardiac catheterization.

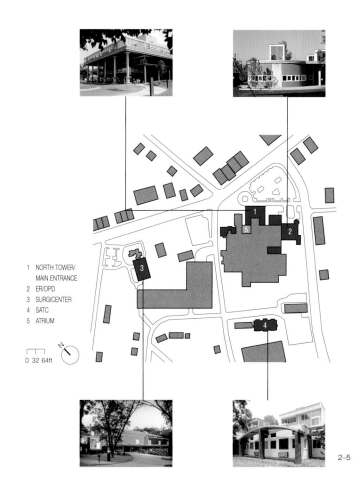

1 NORTH TOWER/
   MAIN ENTRANCE
2 ER/OPD
3 SURGICENTER
4 SATC
5 ATRIUM

0 32 64ft

2–5

6

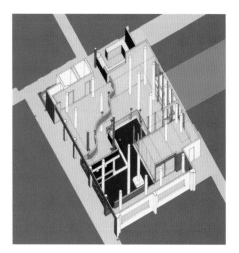

Axonometic of Atrium

7

A multi-story **atrium** at the seam between old and new brings life into the existing hospital.

NORTH TOWER

The demolition of the hospital's east wing made way for a new main elevator with a four-story lobby that serves new and existing programs on all four levels. Circular ceiling wells create pools of light for nurse stations and other active open areas. Light, color, and wood help make the diagnostic and treatment area more inviting and humane.

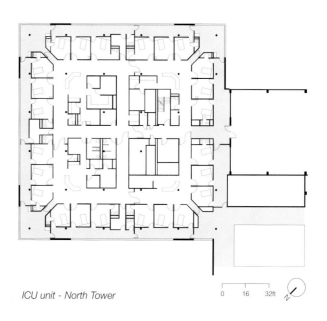

ICU unit - North Tower

0   16   32ft

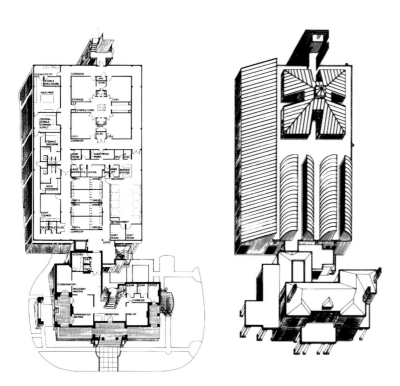

SURGICENTER

The 1910 Talmadge house, one of three built for the Talmadge family on Prince Avenue, was saved from the wrecking ball to become the Surgicenter's reception, waiting, and administration component. Surgery is housed in a new facility attached to the rear of the house. Patients and their companions now arrive at the front of the Talmadge house and leave from the parking level at its rear.

11

12

CORNELL UNIVERSITY MEDICAL COLLEGE
LASDON BIOMEDICAL RESEARCH CENTER

New York, New York

1

The Lasdon Biomedical Research Center prompted two design challenges: first, how can a high-tech building fit into an urban medical center designed in the 1920s; and second, what is the appropriate image relative to the medical center's Southern Avignon Gothic style of architecture, laced with overtones of art deco?

Discussions with Cornell University, New York Hospital, City Planning, and the local community district yielded a design that forges new connections between departments with joint, interdisciplinary research programs. The plan is conceived as a continuation of buildings that extend from 68th to 70th streets. As an infill building with a small floor-plate of 5,200 gross square feet, The Lasdon Building reflects a design approach that is historically respectful, yet distinctly contemporary.

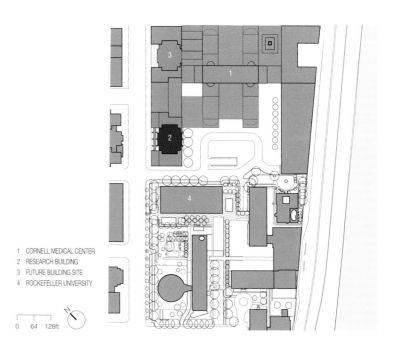

1   CORNELL MEDICAL CENTER
2   RESEARCH BUILDING
3   FUTURE BUILDING SITE
4   ROCKEFELLER UNIVERSITY

0   64   128ft

A **gotham tower** rises between two bookends that define its base.

It? How are these activities inte

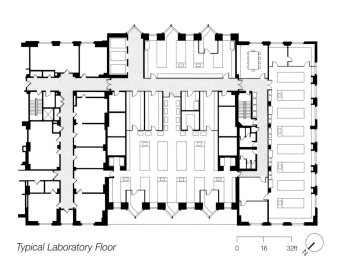

Typical Laboratory Floor

0   16   32ft

For example, the Lasdon architectural massing relates to the New York Presbyterian Hospital Tower, the four corners of which are uninterrupted for their full height, while setbacks cascade on each elevation. This disciplined, sculptural effect emphasizes light, shade, and shadow. Lasdon is classically composed with a base, middle, and top. The base's five Gothic arches connect the first floor with the York Avenue streetscape. The library's large windows allow passersby to observe medical students focused on work, which reinforces the academic image of the medical school. The middle floors house state-of-the-art research laboratories, while the Lasdon top skillfully conceals extensive mechanical equipment.

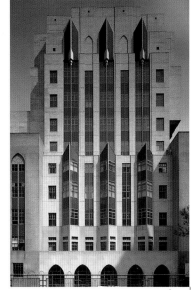

4

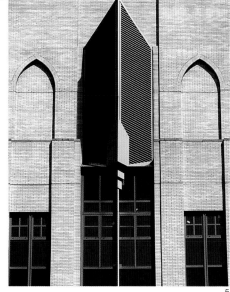

5

upported three-dimensionally? Where is the life of the building, inside and out, day and night, through time? What

An arcade and grade-level library restore the **connection** to the streetscape.

6

GROWTH AND COMPLEXITY

THE JOHNS HOPKINS HOSPITAL I OUTPATIENT CENTER

Baltimore, Maryland

1

The intent of the master plan was to integrate land west of Broadway with the original hospital site, doubling the size of the campus and placing historic buildings at its center. Materials found in the original buildings—red brick, gray-black mortar, and stone trim—are brought to the west campus. The facades, walls, and fences along Broadway and McElderry streets extend the foreground for the three original buildings.

As developed, the Outpatient Center occupies an area west of Broadway directly across from the original hospital. It is divided into two wings in order to reduce the mass of a large building. The Broadway Wing contains related research space and faculty offices, and the McElderry Wing provides the outpatient clinics. Entry to the complex is from Caroline Street to the west. The McElderry turnaround allows access to the McElderry garage, the Outpatient Center, and the new pedestrian mall that is on axis with the dome. Patients simultaneously see the front door, a place to park, and how the two are connected. The covered walkway from the garage to the Outpatient Center first extends an internal concourse through the McElderry Wing,

then reaches under Broadway (where one can enter the Hopkins Metro station), and finally rises via escalators between the Dome and Wilmer Buildings to connect to the hospital's existing concourse system.

1   MCELDERRY STREET MALL
2   OUTPATIENT CENTER
3   BROADWAY WING
4   CONCOURSE HEAD HOUSE
5   FUTURE ONCOLOGY BUILDING
6   FUTURE PARKING
7   PARKING GARAGE
8   MCELDERRY STREET TURN AROUND
9   LOADING DOCK
10 EXISTING CLINICAL BUILDING
11 BROADWAY RESEARCH BUILDING
12 BROADWAY

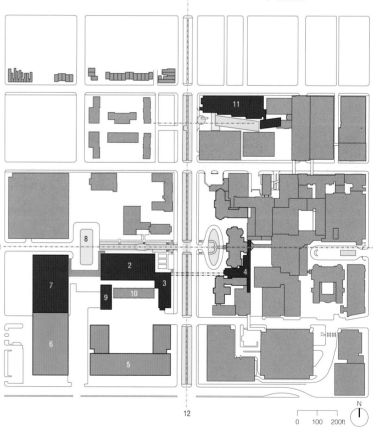

A new pedestrian mall reinforces the **axis** of the original dome building.

82

2

The building block of the Outpatient Center is the exam cluster. It is conceived from the patient's point of view as an improvement over the labyrinthine corridors common in clinics. In addition to exam rooms, the cluster contains a patient bathroom and a private consultation room where doctors can meet with a patient and family members, or where a nurse can provide follow-up instructions while an exam room is being readied for the next patient, or by doctors and students. For doctors, the cluster affords exam rooms close at hand; for nursing staff it is an efficient module, with a place for charting and monitoring vital signs.

The south side of the McElderry Wing is a continuous gallery for clinic reception and waiting. The three pairs of supply and return ducts are located outside the clinic in order not to interrupt the openness of the clinic modules. These clusters also modulate space on each level as they descend from the roof to the ground level.

Patients proceed from the gallery to a waiting area in the core of the clinic, and then to the prototypical exam clusters that run along the north wall of the McElderry Wing.

A prototypical **patient care cluster** was developed for the "ideal" patient visit.

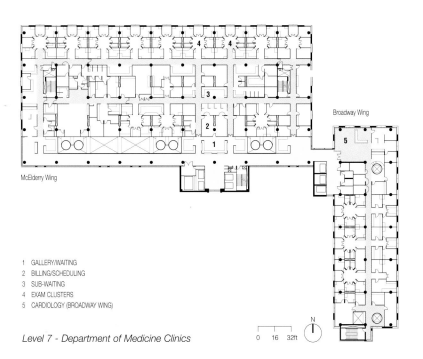

Broadway Wing

McElderry Wing

1 GALLERY/WAITING
2 BILLING/SCHEDULING
3 SUB-WAITING
4 EXAM CLUSTERS
5 CARDIOLOGY (BROADWAY WING)

Level 7 - Department of Medicine Clinics

0   16   32ft

N

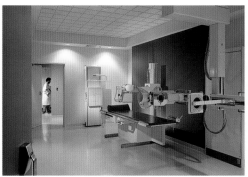

3

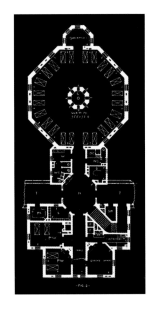

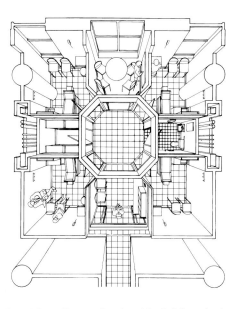

*Original 1889 Patient Ward -
Inspiration for the Cluster*

*Typical Exam Cluster - Developed for Self-Contained
Patient Visit*

4

5

6

The Broadway and McElderry facades have a simplicity and clarity absent in most brick veneer walls. Control and expansion joints divide the brick wall into panels. Windows are recessed to lend a visual thickness to the wall. The building behind the facade consists largely of 100-square-foot rooms. Each consultation room has a large window, and flanking exam rooms each share half of another large window.

Reception desks and seating in waiting areas are framed with painted metal and relate to the exterior glazing frames, vision panels, and interior doors. Translucent laminated glass visually screens computers and other desktop paraphernalia from view of waiting patients, while still allowing natural light.

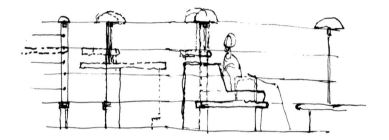

7

8

THE JACKSON LABORATORY | GENETIC RESEARCH BUILDING
Bar Harbor, Maine

1

Completed in 1993, the Jackson Laboratory's new Genetic Research Building is a cutting-edge research facility that provides not only much-needed laboratory space but also offices for principal investigators and post-doctoral researchers, laboratory support space, and storage. Throughout the design process, we sought to provide both an exceptional laboratory and an inspiring space within which to conduct scientific research. Located on Mt. Desert Island, the completed building is respectful of the surrounding natural beauty.

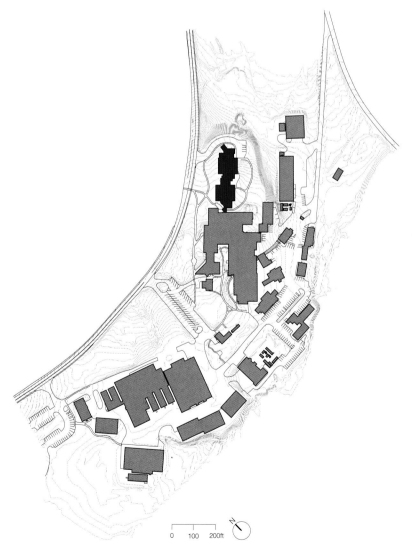

Aggregated building volumes respond to the rural island setting.

88

2

3

4

Offices form the **connective tissue** between the labs.

5

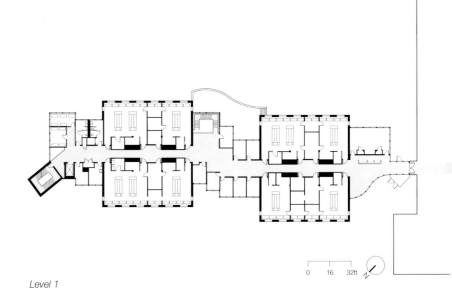

Level 1

0   16   32ft

On the exterior, the volumes are clad in red brick with granite trim, crowned with a standing-seam metal roof. The lab blocks are connected by smaller, flat-roofed volumes with large areas of glass in wood frames to provide maximum light and views for offices, conference rooms, and public areas. The alternating rhythm of laboratory blocks and glassy connectors articulates the building program and lends an appropriate scale to the complex.

The 49,000-square-foot building is organized on four levels. The first floor provides a service entry, storage rooms, and space for mechanical and electrical equipment. The second and third floors are comprised of laboratories, laboratory support spaces, offices, and conference rooms. Four laboratories are grouped together with support spaces to form a laboratory block. The building has two such blocks, identical on the exterior, linked to each other and to the adjoining Snell Building by zones of offices, conference rooms, a lounge, and other support spaces. Mechanical equipment is located on the top floor.

7

6

DUKE UNIVERSITY CAMPUS PLANNING
Durham, North Carolina

1

On the verge of a major program expansion, Duke University retained our firm to evaluate development opportunities in the science precinct of the campus by identifying sites for two large buildings. Working closely with trustees, administrators, and the campus planning committee, several important guidelines were established as essential to achieving a successful campus plan.

First, it was necessary to change the science precinct from one that was vehicular-oriented to one friendly to pedestrians. Large parking areas and access roads were moved from the heart of the precinct to the periphery of the campus. (See area dotted in red.)

Second, it was desirable to transform the science precinct from a landscape of isolated buildings (some as far apart as 500 feet) to a community of more closely sited buildings. To create opportunities for people to work together, share knowledge, and pool resources (thus promoting the university's mission of interdisciplinary science), new footprints "reach out and touch" other buildings. New facilities were limited to four stories.

Third, to strengthen the identity of the science precinct and its sense of place, new courtyard spaces, pathways, and landscaping were created. These elements have been perceived historically as the finest attributes of American college campuses. The plan now allows students, faculty, staff, and visitors to interact and experience this scholarly environment in a lushly landscaped setting. The result is a new sense of unity and dignity in the science precinct, complementing the arts and humanities precinct of Duke's historic campus.

0 100 200ft

■ BUILT PROJECT
▨ PLANNED PROJECT

1 LEVINE SCIENCE RESEARCH CENTER
2 SOUTH QUADRANGLE, BIOLOGY, AND
   CHEMISTRY BUILDINGS
3 MEDICAL SCIENCE RESEARCH BUILDING
4 FUTURE MEDICAL SCIENCE
   RESEARCH BUILDINGS
5 DUKE UNIVERSITY EYE CENTER
6 MEDICAL CENTER LIBRARY

By closing science drive, the sciences are **connected** to the main campus.

DUKE UNIVERSITY I LEVINE SCIENCE RESEARCH CENTER

Durham, North Carolina

1

The new science center is designed to encourage interaction among scientists from across the university. Duke's renowned Collegiate Gothic campus, with its courtyards and gray stone cladding, inspired the architecture of the new science research center.

The building defines two new campus spaces, the school for the environment courtyard and the main quad. An 800-foot-long arcade connects the two spaces with a ground level cafe acting as a filter between the two courtyards. Service access is shielded from the campus along the north face of the building.

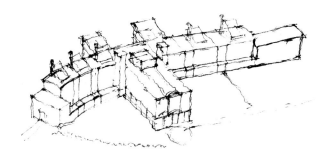

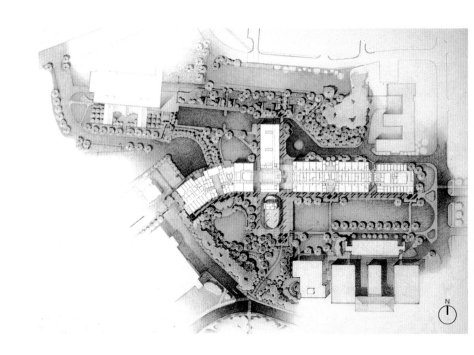

Creating a **campus for the sciences**, the building offers a variety of outdoor and campus green sp

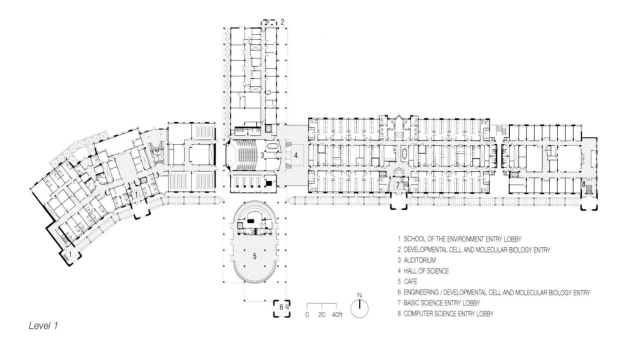

Level 1

1 SCHOOL OF THE ENVIRONMENT ENTRY LOBBY
2 DEVELOPMENTAL CELL AND MOLECULAR BIOLOGY ENTRY
3 AUDITORIUM
4 HALL OF SCIENCE
5 CAFE
6 ENGINEERING / DEVELOPMENTAL CELL AND MOLECULAR BIOLOGY ENTRY
7 BASIC SCIENCE ENTRY LOBBY
8 COMPUTER SCIENCE ENTRY LOBBY

The center includes a 300-seat auditorium and conference rooms. Facilities are designed to promote the exchange of ideas through university-wide, national, and international seminars and conferences. All of Duke's science departments meet and merge at the main entrance lobby, a grand space known as the "Hall of Science," which provides the shared amenities of a cafe, conference

Each department within the building has its own **identity** and entrance.

rooms, informal lounges, and a central stair. The auditorium and science departments each have their own entry off this central space. The auditorium entry located off the main staircase mid-landing is the most prominent threshold in the Hall of Science. A central cafe serves as a daily meeting place for faculty, students, and visiting scholars from both the center and the science and engineering buildings surrounding it.

2

pported three-dimensionally? What is the life of the building,

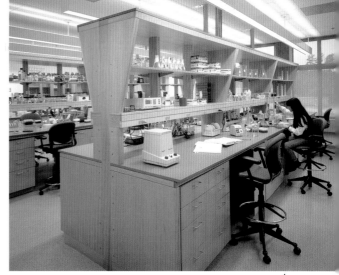

3

4

6

5

The exterior's beige and gray pre-cast concrete accented by blue-painted steel evokes the flavor of Duke's main campus. Additionally, the use of clear glass windows, entrance towers, grouped chimneys, and other Gothic-inspired elements reinforce this connection. Landscape elements such as low stone walls and plantings help meld the new building with the existing science buildings. The new center's configuration on the site creates private pockets of outdoor space, some of which can be used as outdoor classrooms.

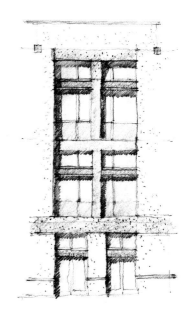

BIOGEN, INC I BIOGEN BUILDINGS 6, 8, AND 9

Cambridge, Massachusetts

1

Located in Cambridge's Kendall Square, Biogen's new facilities constitute a new urban corporate campus. One of the project's goals was to plan for future growth and expansion while at the same time creating an identity and image consistent throughout the complex. The tight site, which is bisected by an existing parking garage, was analyzed to determine the most efficient land use. The site was developed in a two-phase plan that uses L-shaped courtyard buildings as the primary building block for the campus. These three buildings encompass approximately 650,000 square feet.

BIO 8 RESEARCH BUILDING

The five-story Bio 8 Process Development and Research Building includes laboratories, offices, a cafe, and flexible meeting spaces. The plan revolves about a central core with corridors radiating from this hub and terminating in open resource libraries. All laboratories and offices have natural light. A vivarium and mechanical and support spaces are in the basement. Outside, the building's angular form reflects a response to the melding of two urban grids that overlap on the site. The building's L-shape encloses a courtyard.

1 BIO 9, 2004 (est.)
2 BIO 8, 2001
3 BIO 1—RENOVATION
4 BIO 2—RENOVATION
5 BIO 6A—FUTURE BUILDING
6 BIO 6—1995
7 BIO 7—RENOVATION
8 BIO 4—RENOVATION

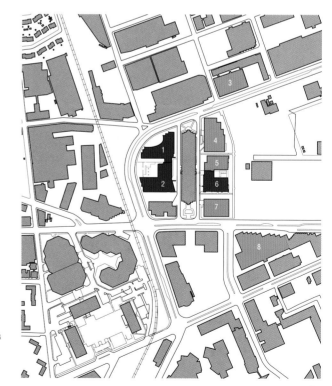

An **urban** site is transformed to accommodate a corporate campus.

100

2

3

4

The architecture promotes **interaction** within and between buildings.

BIO 6 RESEARCH FACILITY

The Bio 6 Research Facility includes two floors of biology research laboratories, one floor of chemistry research laboratories, and two floors of offices, which can be converted into laboratories at a later date. The overall massing and architectural articulation of the building are derived directly from its internal organization. From the core (clad in brick to match the company's existing facility) extend three curtain-walled elevations that reflect the laboratory functions on the upper five floors. Different programmatic areas and their inter-relationships are expressed through the fenestration.

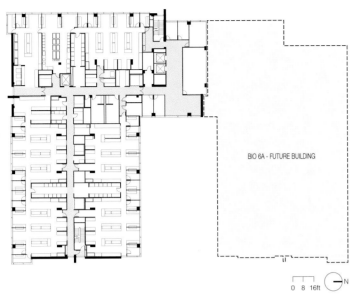

Bio 6 - Floor Plan

BIO 6A - FUTURE BUILDING

0 8 16ft   N

6

5

BIO 9 RESEARCH BUILDING

Finally, the Bio 9 Research Building helps
to establish the north and east edges of
the Biogen campus. The 205,000-square-
foot facility houses programs that constitute a mix of chemistry and biology research. The program also includes such
amenities as conference/seminar rooms,
a fitness club, and a full-service cafeteria.

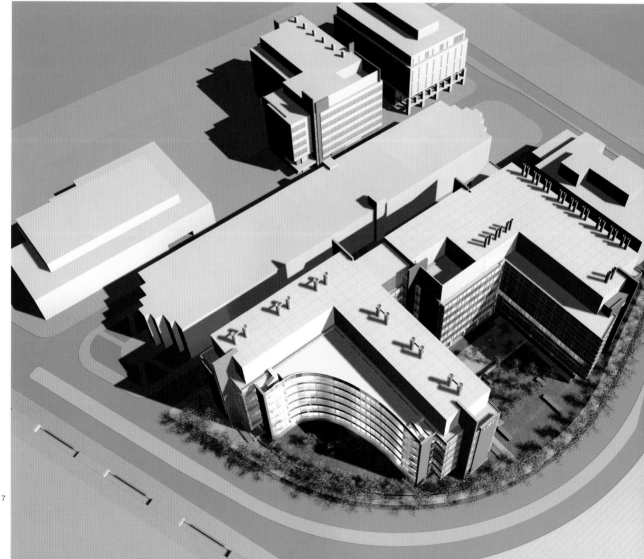

7

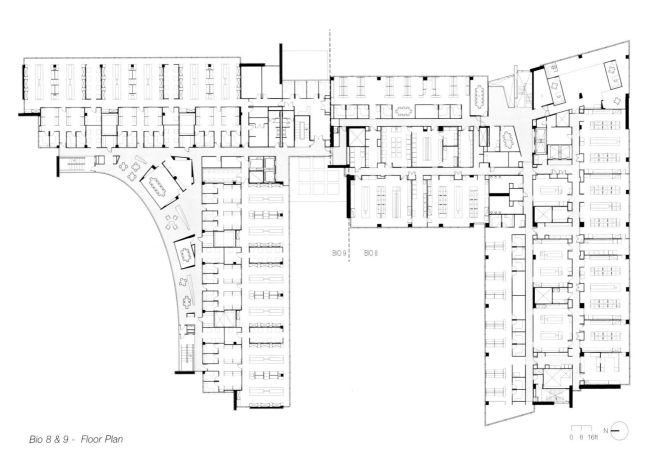

Bio 8 & 9 - Floor Plan

BIO 9   BIO 8

0   8   16ft   N

1

The Chemistry Building at Vanderbilt University provides new facilities for synthetic chemistry teaching and research. It is located at the center of the 1960s Stevenson Science Center—a simple composition of five loft-like rectangular solids. The new building's constrained site, the required adjacency to the existing chemistry facilities, and the desire to preserve the lovely Magnolia Courtyard all guided its placement at the center of the complex in space above the existing lecture hall building and the below-grade science library. The lecture hall building is subsumed in the base of the much larger new building, which is now the focal point for the Science Center.

1 NEW CHEMISTRY BUILDING
2 STEVENSON SCIENCE CENTER

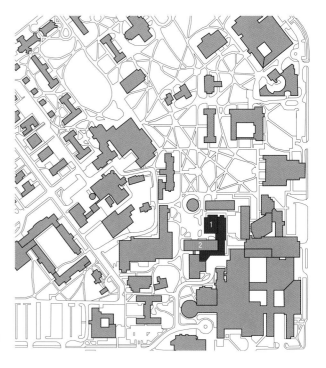

0 64 128ft

N

Animated roof forms create identity within a bleak 1960s science precinct.

2

The building's forms and facades represent the programmatic elements they serve. The laboratories are boxy Cartesian volumes with rigorous brick facades and large punched windows. In contrast, the office, conference, entry, and circulation areas are faced in precast concrete and curtain wall, freely sculpted. Stair and elevator cores are strong vertical elements faced in limestone, visible on the interior and projecting through the roof. The Chemistry Building utilizes the language and methodology of the Stevenson Science Center, while adding a sense of playfulness.

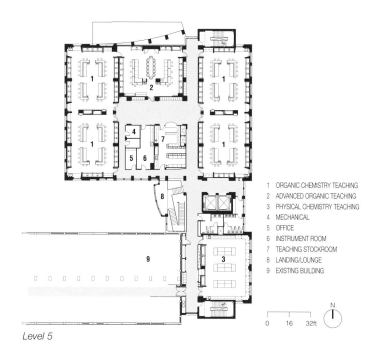

1 ORGANIC CHEMISTRY TEACHING
2 ADVANCED ORGANIC TEACHING
3 PHYSICAL CHEMISTRY TEACHING
4 MECHANICAL
5 OFFICE
6 INSTRUMENT ROOM
7 TEACHING STOCKROOM
8 LANDING/LOUNGE
9 EXISTING BUILDING

0   16   32ft   N

Level 5

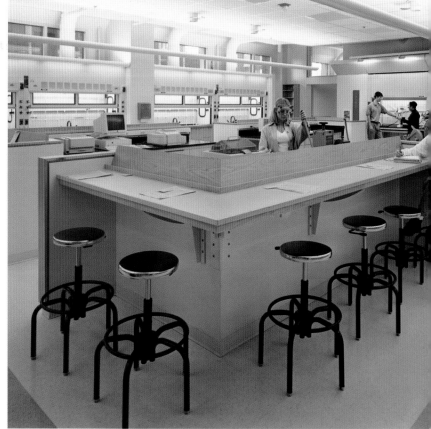

3

4

A bridge building **spans** two existing lecture halls.

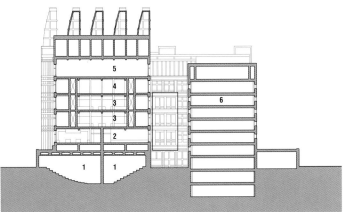

1 EXISTING LECTURE HALLS
2 ADMINISTRATION
3 RESEARCH LABS
4 TEACHING LABS
5 MECHANICAL
6 EXISTING BUILDING

With the first full floor of teaching laboratories located 24 feet above grade, the open stair to this level has a large landing that functions as a rest area, study lounge, and place of interaction for students and faculty.

Among the technical, programmatic, and design challenges, the large ventilation systems required to serve 220 fume hoods became an element in the expression of the building. The result was a 38-foot-high penthouse and five sail-shaped exhaust stacks each 60 feet high.

YALE UNIVERSITY I 350 EDWARDS STREET

New Haven, Connecticut

1

This new facility centralizes all materials handling for the Science Hill section of the Yale University campus. The building is composed of two floors set into the hillside, with faculty and staff access at the upper level and separate loading docks at the lower level. The building uses the hill to its advantage on a very narrow site, and is slightly angled to provide access to both loading docks. This geometry also allows truck and service access to other buildings within the complex.

The scale of the building relates to the smaller residential buildings on Edwards Street. The building's access and proximity to Edwards Street provides an opportunity to extend the residential scale and grid into the academic block and to soften the edge between the neighborhood and the campus.

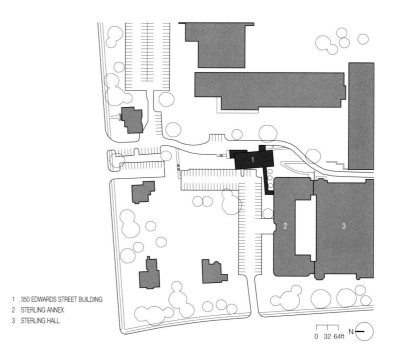

1   350 EDWARDS STREET BUILDING
2   STERLING ANNEX
3   STERLING HALL

0 32 64ft   N

A **contextual building** in a modern context.

2

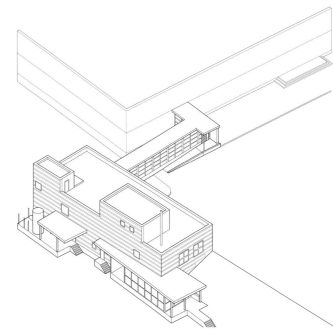

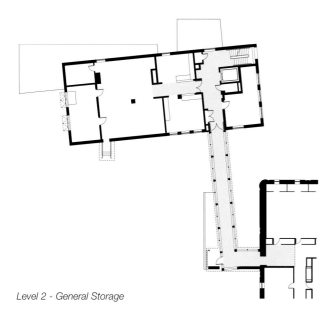

Level 2 - General Storage

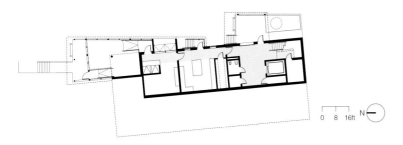

0 8 16ft N

Level 1 - Loading Dock

3

The stair tower and the mechanical room modulate the simple mass of the masonry volume. In contrast to the building mass, the canopies align with the campus grid, canting the loading docks toward the driveway. The few punched openings are windows, vents, and louvers. Thin brownstone banding visually integrates these seemingly random openings and provides scale and order to an otherwise simple brick building. The highly textured cut on the brownstone, contrasting with the reflective machine finish of the iron-spot brick, changes appearance depending on the time of day and the quality of light on its surface. (The material was acquired from the same quarry that supplied Yale with brownstone in the early 20th century.) The mix of the brick was adjusted to match the material of the adjacent building.

Brownstone from a reopened quarry dignifies a typically **back-of-house** facility.

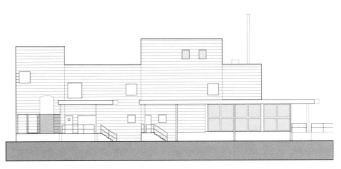

South Elevation

East Elevation

CARNEGIE MELLON UNIVERSITY | ROBERTS ENGINEERING HALL

Pittsburgh, Pennsylvania

1

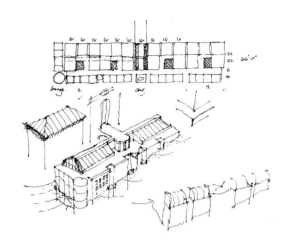

This building becomes a base to historic Hamerschlag Hall, the symbol for Carnegie Mellon University. The steep site, which slopes into a hollow, placed the building adjacent to the train line that once brought coal to Hamerschlag's basement steam plant and ornate stack. Both the rail and the steam plant were long ago retired.

The design extends the patterns and rhythms found in campus architect Henry Hornbostel's work from the early 20th century. A sketch on the opposite page reveals Hornbostel's unexpected intention for the ravine site.

The base of tinted concrete blends with the campus brick. The roof is sloped metal set just below the main windows of Hamerschlag and houses the main conference room in its rounded form. The electronics materials research laboratories are found in concrete bays that are evenly modulated.

1 ROBERTS ENGINEERING HALL
2 HAMERSCHLAG HALL

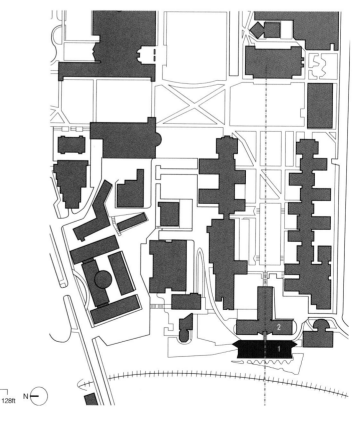

0   64 128ft   N

A found site located within the hillside **completes a campus axis.**

114

te patterns of space and circulation that transform its se   past, pr

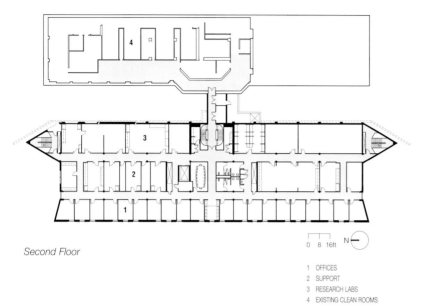

Second Floor

0 8 16ft   N

1 OFFICES
2 SUPPORT
3 RESEARCH LABS
4 EXISTING CLEAN ROOMS

The organization of spaces along the hillside locates places for people (such as offices) by the windows (where they can enjoy light and views) and sensitive laboratories into the hill closer to Hamerschlag. Stairwells become vessels of natural light, delivering it to the lower levels of laboratories.

The mid-floor laboratories extending under a roadway into the Clean Room of Hamerschlag Hall—a space once occupied by a steam plant—make an important connection in this 72,000-square-foot building. Above the roadway, the main lobby links the two buildings, celebrates the vista of the historic tower, and provides natural light into the three-story stair that links the lobby to laboratories and clean rooms.

5

6

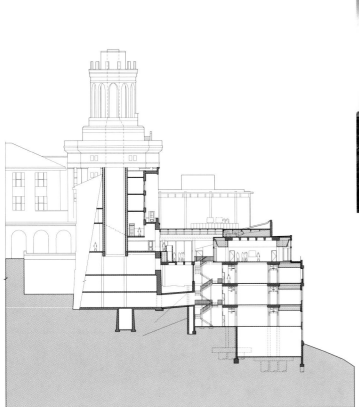

HENRIETTA D. GOODALL HOSPITAL I AMBULATORY SURGICAL UNIT
Sanford, Maine

This addition to a 1920s hospital in rural Maine includes an underground ambulatory surgical unit and a new entrance lobby. The project is part of a larger plan that shifts the main entrance from the side of a nondescript 1960s addition back toward the geometric center of the campus. The new addition works to heighten the importance of the original 1920s-era structures, recapturing the symbolic heart of the campus.

The sculpting of form to bring light into the patient spaces is the central theme of the design. The existing below-grade location of the surgical suite and the need for an immediately adjacent ambulatory surgical unit called for an innovative approach to give the building an above-ground presence and to bring natural light into patient recovery rooms.

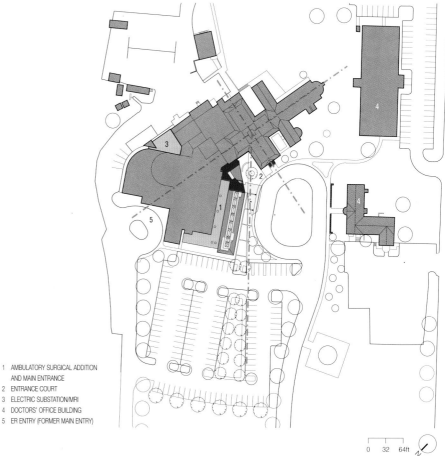

1   AMBULATORY SURGICAL ADDITION
    AND MAIN ENTRANCE
2   ENTRANCE COURT
3   ELECTRIC SUBSTATION/MRI
4   DOCTORS' OFFICE BUILDING
5   ER ENTRY (FORMER MAIN ENTRY)

0   32   64ft

Restores the original entry sequence through a **reinterpreted** form.

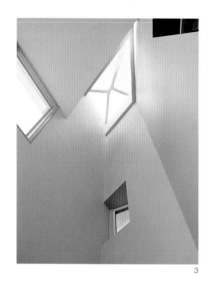

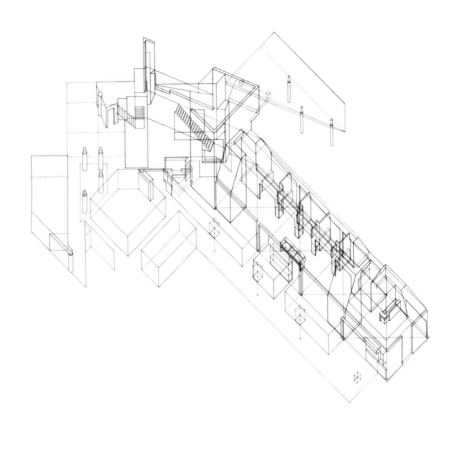

Reclaims space, light, and volume to define a **primordial shelter** for heali

The massing is of two distinct forms. The first is a skewed masonry block containing a three-story entrance lobby, roughly symmetrical, with a brick pavilion at the far side of the 1928 main building. The second is an innovative prism-like block, inspired by the Mansard roofs of the old building. The prism form draws natural light into the below-grade ambulatory surgical unit—with a slate garden wall that one can touch. The distinctive roof is part potato barn, part sculpture, and part primordial shelter for healing.

Forms evolve from a subtractive massing strategy, which transforms the Mansard roof profile of the existing building. The roof and its tactile materials are brought down to grade, resulting in a varied section responding to site geometry and program. The building mass is then explored as poché.

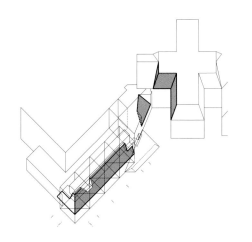

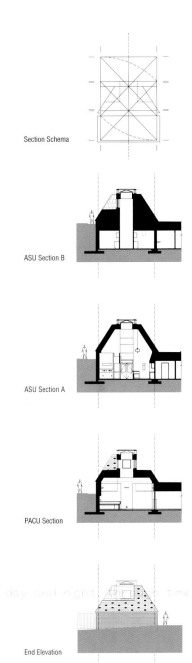

Section Schema

ASU Section B

ASU Section A

PACU Section

End Elevation

5

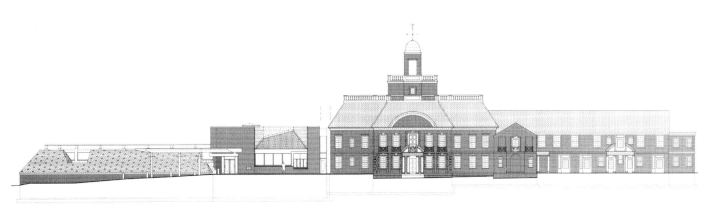

VETERANS AFFAIRS MEDICAL CENTER
AMBULATORY CARE ADDITION AND RENOVATION

Providence, Rhode Island

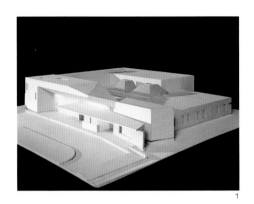

1

Located on the outskirts of Providence, this project's immediate surroundings include residential and industrial buildings. The existing Medical Center is a seven-story brick building with several rambling additions, woven together by meandering circulation routes. The new design creates a hierarchy of circulation, providing a clear sense of entry, accessed by a new arrival sequence from the major road that bounds the site.

A new drive leads to a two-story entry pavilion clad in pre-oxidized copper panels. Visually separate from the rambling brick masses of the hospital campus, the contemporary use of the material suggests the time-honored tradition of using copper cupolas, domes, and dormers to announce the entry to important civic and collegiate buildings. The addition's hilltop location and prominence provide a distinguished entry without resorting to a symmetrical composition.

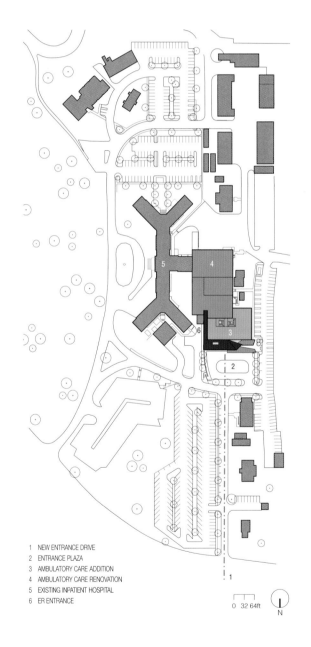

1 NEW ENTRANCE DRIVE
2 ENTRANCE PLAZA
3 AMBULATORY CARE ADDITION
4 AMBULATORY CARE RENOVATION
5 EXISTING INPATIENT HOSPITAL
6 ER ENTRANCE

0 32 64ft

N

A bold new entrance sequence and **portal** for the hospital.

2

Color is both a catalyst and an urban design element that brings scale and a larger sense of organization to an extremely large floor plate. Color reinforces the primary public seams on the ground plane while spatial layering of the project brings the dynamic geometry of the lobby into the clinic's interior, breaks up lengthy corridors, and enlivens the building's existing static geometry.

The addition and renovation create two primary-care firms with a specialist firm between them for the ease of consultations and referrals. Each firm contains a ring of exam/office spaces surrounding a private waiting area that also functions as a light court. Clinic reception is located at the entry to the ring's entry at the main corridor, while staff access to the exam/office areas is via a secondary perimeter corridor.

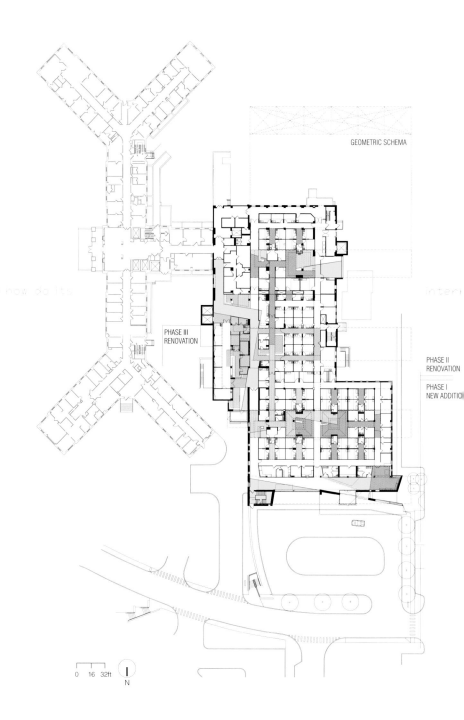

GEOMETRIC SCHEMA

PHASE III RENOVATION

PHASE II RENOVATION

PHASE I NEW ADDITION

0   16   32ft

N

3

Clustered exam **neighborhoods** have become a national primary care prototype for the VA.

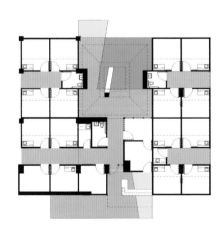

4

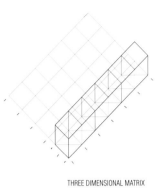

THREE DIMENSIONAL MATRIX

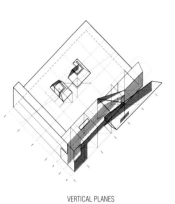

VERTICAL PLANES

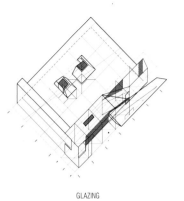

GLAZING

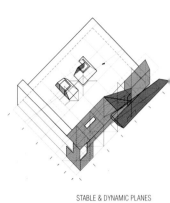

STABLE & DYNAMIC PLANES

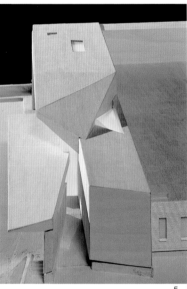

5

The form of the entrance pavilion results from the superimposition of two distinct systems. The conceptual order of a linearly arranged 26-foot cube is carved away by the functional system of diagonal circulation through the entrance pavilion.

In connecting the geometry of the site to the Ambulatory Care facility, the formal order is modified by site lines and movement. Points of intersection of the "ideal" and "functional" orders are punctuated by natural light.

6

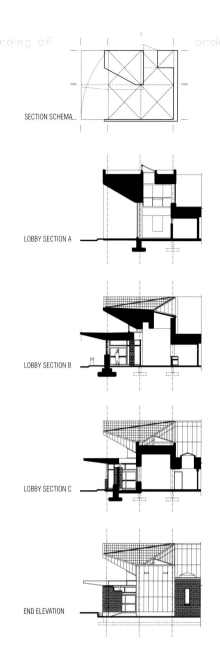

SECTION SCHEMA

LOBBY SECTION A

LOBBY SECTION B

LOBBY SECTION C

END ELEVATION

7

8

COLLEGE OF WOOSTER | SEVERANCE CHEMISTRY ADDITION

Wooster, Ohio

1

Severance Hall, built in 1902 as the home of the Chemistry Department at this liberal arts college, was outdated and badly in need of repair. Because of its prominent location and architectural value, the college chose to restore and enlarge this masonry and heavy-timber structure to provide new teaching laboratories, independent study research laboratories, lecture areas, and faculty offices.

The building form, particularly the main entrance, recognizes and responds to new patterns of pedestrian traffic from nearby housing, athletic facilities, the science library, and the student center. Placed on the east side of the existing structure, the addition creates a major new entrance opposite the science library and student pathway with a dramatic two-story entry lobby as its organizing feature. Additional enhancements include a shared student lounge and a landscaped garden between Severance and the adjacent biology building.

The massing and detailing of buff colored brick and limestone strongly relates to Wooster's Jacobean architectural style. The new building utilizes three slightly different colors of brick, as well as a darker header and specially shaped details to echo the composition of the older structure and knit the two facades together.

1 NEW CHEMISTRY ADDITION
2 CHEMISTRY RENOVATIONS
3 BIOLOGY

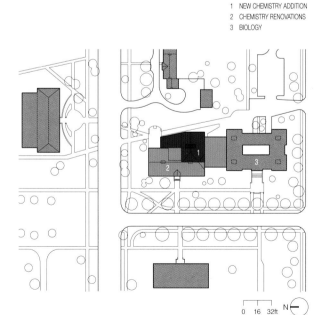

0   16   32ft   N

The addition retains the identity of the original structure on a **prominent site**

2

ain campus walk. ...of space and circulation that transform its se... ...the pas...

129

Shared research laboratories promote faculty and student **interaction**.

4

The entire building offers very tall floor heights with abundant natural light in nearly all spaces. The new labs bridge the old and the new structures seamlessly, with the older exterior wall surface acting as a permeable membrane between laboratories. Open passageways accommodate flexibility in class sizes and teaching methods. Exposed ceilings highlight the steel framing and decking as a contemporary interpretation of the existing heavy timber and wood decking. Mechanical systems exposed in these overhead spaces reveal the technology required to support chemistry teaching.

5

of the building, inside and out, day and night, through time? What p

6

1 NEW CONSTRUCTION
2 RENOVATION

Level 2

0   16   32ft   N

HARVARD SCHOOL OF PUBLIC HEALTH
FRANCOIS-XAVIER BAGNOUD BUILDING

Boston, Massachusetts

1

The Francois-Xavier Bagnoud (FXB) Building is located on Huntington Avenue in Boston, a major urban axis in the city. The eight-story, 105,000-square-foot building houses biomedical research laboratories for AIDS research.

This project faced three major design challenges. First, the site—a slender, triangular lot—was constrained by the diagonal intersection of Huntington Avenue and adjacent buildings. The architecture of the new building accommodates the geometry of the street as well as the existing buildings. When viewed from the east, the cantilevered roof line of the entry lobby reinforces the angular shape of the site, providing a distinguishing and arresting feature on the street.

Second, the building needed to project an updated image for the school. The solution reinforces the street edge and provides a vibrant new entrance. This entry portal acts as a forecourt to the varied research activities happening behind the street wall.

Third, the building needed to harmonize with existing school buildings. Horizontal massing and a palette of warm materials help to achieve this result. The granite base, stainless steel railings and accents, and buff-colored precast panels reflect the urban context.

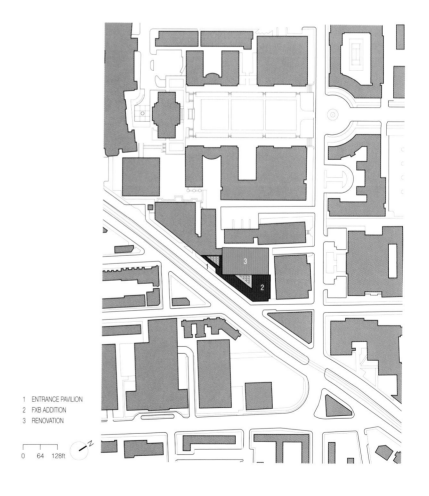

1 ENTRANCE PAVILION
2 FXB ADDITION
3 RENOVATION

0   64   128ft

A complex site geometry dictates the building form to create a **new identity** and front

132

2

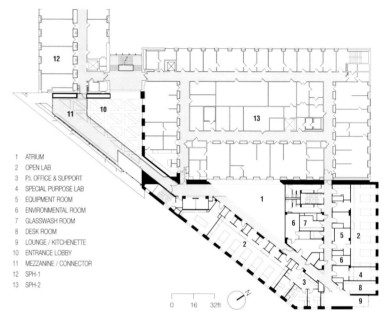

1 ATRIUM
2 OPEN LAB
3 P.I. OFFICE & SUPPORT
4 SPECIAL PURPOSE LAB
5 EQUIPMENT ROOM
6 ENVIRONMENTAL ROOM
7 GLASSWASH ROOM
8 DESK ROOM
9 LOUNGE / KITCHENETTE
10 ENTRANCE LOBBY
11 MEZZANINE / CONNECTOR
12 SPH-1
13 SPH-2

0   16   32ft

Level 2

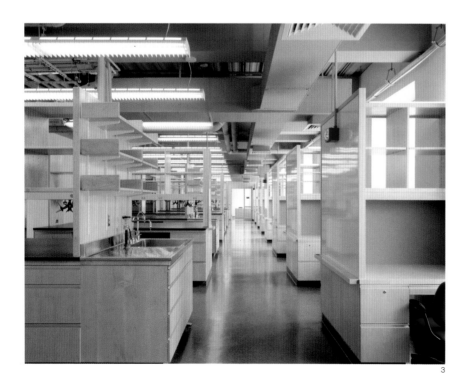

3

The siting of the building knits together two adjacent laboratory buildings (SPH-1 and SPH-2) through a multi-story public lobby and atrium, creating a new center for research and unifying the four-building complex. The atrium also provides orientation and delivers natural light to the existing laboratories.

ch super block.

4

5

SEOUL NATIONAL UNIVERSITY I INTERNATIONAL VACCINE INSTITUTE

Seoul, Korea

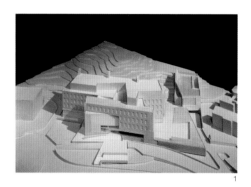

1

The International Vaccine Institute, a 180,000-square-foot facility at Seoul National University, was awarded through an international design competition. Established by a collaboration of the United Nations Development Program, the Korean government, and the University, it supports vaccine research for childhood diseases. It is the largest facility of its type in the world.

The complex is carefully sited to create strong ties with the mountainous landscape, while reinforcing a site axis through the complex to Kwanak Mountain. The building form is fractured along an existing footpath that extends through the site to a temple on top of the mountain. Clear functional divisions separate the administration, research, and production areas, all expressed in the building's architectural forms. Terraced gardens and a plaza link them together, much in the tradition of Korean landscape design.

The massing is articulated as three layers and volumes that can be read as one building or several. An intricate system of site walls, terraces, and gardens links the forms together, cradling the mountainous landscape.

The three massing layers each have diverse contents: the entrance pavilion consists of the library and offices/apartments for visiting faculty; a research lab block includes labs and offices for resident faculty; while a pilot production plant is contained in the third. Below the terrace that links the forms are an animal facility, parking garage, and a secure buildings services area.

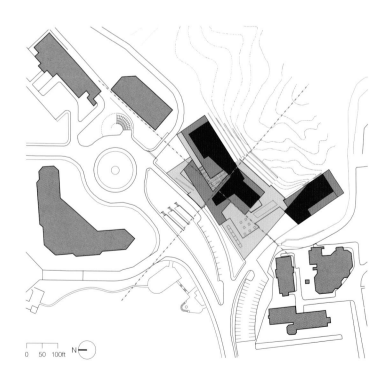

0   50   100ft   N

Forms are transformed by a **complex topography**, embracing the geometry of the mountains.

136

2

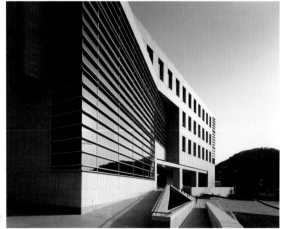

3

1 CONFERENCE CENTER
2 ADMINISTRATION
3 PILOT PLANT
4 TERRACE GARDEN
5 LOADING DOCK (BELOW)
6 LIBRARY
7 RESEARCH LAB

Level 1

Level 2

0   16 32ft

4

5

Generous public spaces enhance the scientific culture of the institute. Horizontal and vertical openness foster a communal spirit centered on the atrium and also provide natural light to labs and offices. Highly public areas such as the conference center and library are entered from the ground floor, while highly restricted research areas float above the main floor. These two distinct areas are visually connected (yet secure) by a communicating stair suspended above the lobby.

The T-shaped atrium and lobby spaces are bi-directional, oriented both east-west and north-south, linked with a dramatic sloping skylight over the entire expanse and visually connected to the landscape across both axes.

7

6

ection, three-dimensionally? What is

Exterior fenestration is composed of two systems: glass and Korean granite. The indigenous granite is quarried locally to give the building the natural color of the stone found on the nearby mountains—a giant outcropping of sorts. Stone is used to reflect the planar qualities of the building's faceted massing and is carved with articulated detail at the intersections of the elements. Simple rectangular punched window openings are used for all labs and offices. Larger expanses of window wall express public spaces in the building, such as the library, the conference center, and the atrium.

All research labs are oriented toward the mountains and nature, while all the exterior offices face the city. The large conference rooms cantilevered off the east end of the building face the university.

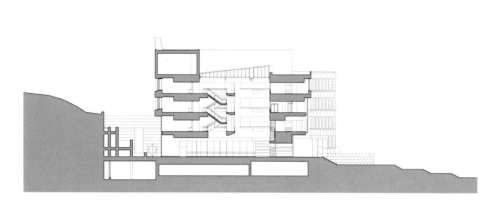

Cross Sections

8

9

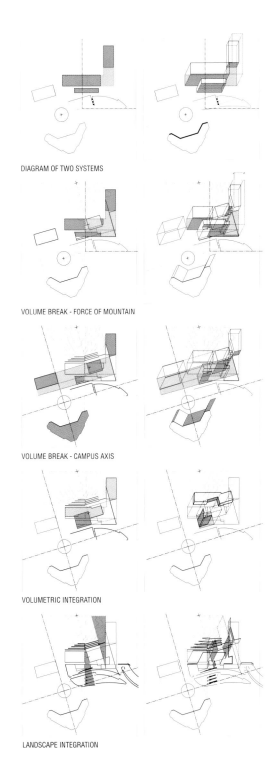

DIAGRAM OF TWO SYSTEMS

VOLUME BREAK - FORCE OF MOUNTAIN

VOLUME BREAK - CAMPUS AXIS

VOLUMETRIC INTEGRATION

LANDSCAPE INTEGRATION

10

CREATING CAMPUS COMMUNITY

MIDDLEBURY COLLEGE I BICENTENNIAL HALL
Middlebury, Vermont

1

Middlebury's science departments embrace the idea that experimentation and discovery are at the heart of the liberal arts experience. With this driving force in mind, the client challenged us to bring together all of the science disciplines into a large new building.

The building's steeply sloped site defines the northwest edge of the campus and extends the boundaries of the academic precinct to create a new focal point.

The building contains four stone wings that radiate from a five-story interior "Great Hall." This central space at the heart of the building is for study, meeting, and informal learning. From the Great Hall, dramatic exterior views to the north and west bring the surrounding Vermont countryside into the building. The connection between the building and the site is reinforced through the use of slate flooring, warm red oak wall panels, and abundant natural light.

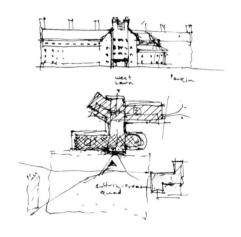

2

Extends **academic fabric** to a new campus boundary.

3

Sixteen different undergraduate programs are housed in an **academic loft**.

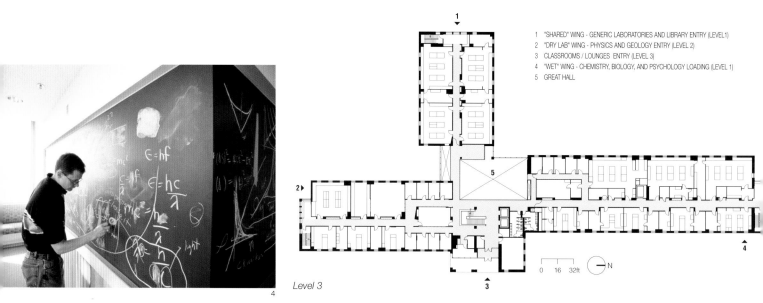

1 "SHARED" WING - GENERIC LABORATORIES AND LIBRARY ENTRY (LEVEL1)
2 "DRY LAB" WING - PHYSICS AND GEOLOGY ENTRY (LEVEL 2)
3 CLASSROOMS / LOUNGES ENTRY (LEVEL 3)
4 "WET" WING - CHEMISTRY, BIOLOGY, AND PSYCHOLOGY LOADING (LEVEL 1)
5 GREAT HALL

Level 3

4

146

The classroom and lab spaces are organized into the four wings that extend from the Great Hall. The north wing contains the "wet sciences," including chemistry, biochemistry, biology, psychology, and a shared animal facility. Dry functions are housed in the south wing and include labs and classrooms for physics, geology, geography, and common lecture halls. A small east wing contains three flat-floor classrooms and three informal learning spaces. The west wing, or "Shared Wing", contains 12 generic laboratories that can be configured for multiple users and changes in curriculum, enrollment, and teaching methods.

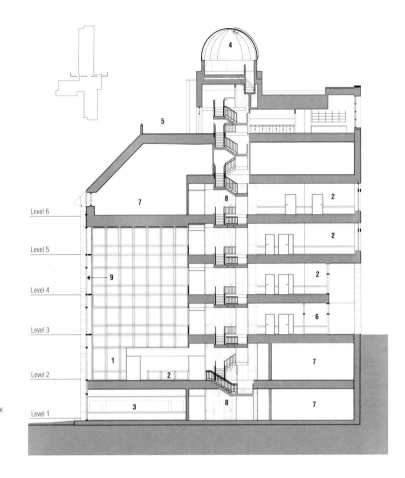

1 GREAT HALL
2 INFORMAL LEARNING
3 CLASSROOM
4 OBSERVATORY DOME
5 ROOF / OBSERVATION DECK
6 EAST ENTRY
7 MECHANICAL
8 ELEVATOR LOBBY
9 WEST WINDOW

5

The exterior is reminiscent of New England mill buildings—the precedent for the 18th century buildings on the College's Old Stone Row. The exterior is clad with both dressed and rough-cut Adair and Indiana limestones, interspersed with expanses of glass curtainwall. The roof is slate. The exterior reflects the traditional vernacular of this quintessential New England campus. The interior finishes in public areas are natural wood and slate.

This new facility demonstrates Middlebury's leadership in environmentally sensitive buildings through its healthy balance of sustainable technologies, their costs, and their benefits. The new facility is the largest academic structure in the country to contain "green-certified" timber, harvested and processed through ecologically sensitive means.

6

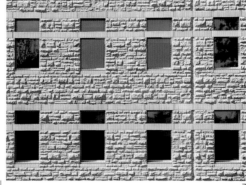
7

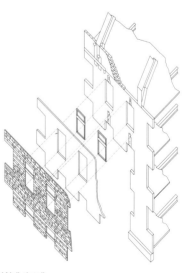

Wall detail

8

WASHINGTON AND LEE UNIVERSITY
SCIENCE CENTER AND SORORITY HOUSING

Lexington, Virginia

1

SCIENCE CENTER

Washington and Lee University, a liberal
arts school of 2,000 students, was
founded in 1749 and is the sixth oldest
institution of higher education in the
country. The front campus is a designated
National Historic Landmark. Our two
projects acknowledge that history while
establishing their own presence in a
current time and place.

The Science Center strengthens the
school's undergraduate science program
with major improvements to two existing
science buildings and construction of a
new addition that creates a single complex. The two existing buildings, Howe
and Parmly Halls, define the northwest
corner of the academic campus.
Stemmons Plaza, a central pedestrian
spine to the rear of the original historic
buildings, stops short of the eastern edge,
Dupont Hall, and does not address the
two science buildings. The new addition
creates a symbolic entrance to the complex, unites the two buildings, and addresses Stemmons Plaza.

1 SCIENCE CENTER ADDITION
2 HOWE HALL SCIENCE CENTER RENOVATION
3 PARMLY HALL SCIENCE CENTER RENOVATION
4 DUPONT HALL (PORTICO ADDITION)
5 SORORITY HOUSING

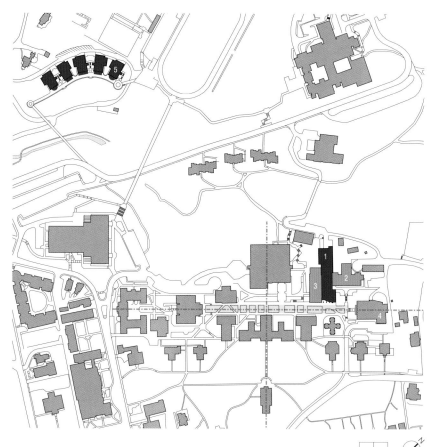

The science center completes the definition of the **historic mall**.

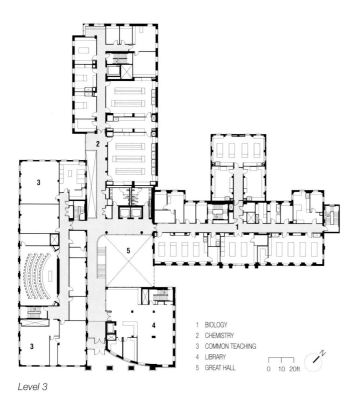

Level 3

1 BIOLOGY
2 CHEMISTRY
3 COMMON TEACHING
4 LIBRARY
5 GREAT HALL

0 10 20ft

The new Science Center is organized along a central circulation spine and includes a "Great Hall" from which students can access the six science departments. This hub and spoke concept gives each of the six science departments a front door on the Great Hall. The library's location at the main entry makes it the symbolic and literal focus of the Center and Great Hall.

The classical revival architecture of the campus presented a challenge: how to harmonize the new facility with the existing character of the campus while expressing the Science Center as a technologically advanced building that embraces the future. A symmetrical and classically detailed temple facade fronts an asymmetrical and curving brick wall that hints at a more contemporary interior beyond. The skylit spine preserves the facades of the existing buildings as an interior arcade leading past the library's front door to the Great Hall.

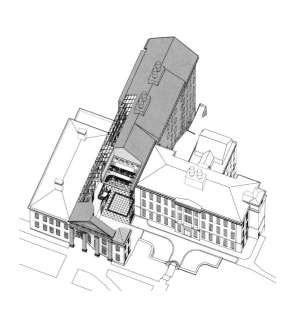

2

3

4

lationships between teaching and research

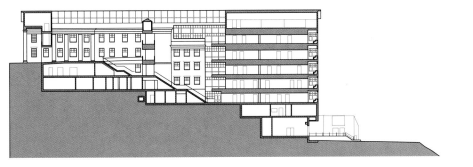

SORORITY HOUSING

The planning and design of the sorority complex was based on the notion of "community": the community of each sorority chapter (house), the community of the collective sorority life on campus (site plan), and finally as part of the greater Washington and Lee academic communities (contextual planning and design).

As the original buildings on the historic campus are unified along the "Colonnade" overlooking a large lawn, the sorority houses are sited along a pedestrian circulation path. This extension of the existing classic revival style of the historic campus provides a continuum—a link across the natural boundaries to the north side of the campus.

We worked with members of all the sorority chapters to establish a standard program that could then be tailored to the individual characteristics and "secrets" of the particular national chapters.

5

6

FUTURE 6TH HOUSE   KKΓ   KΔ   ΠΒΦ   KAΘ   XΩ

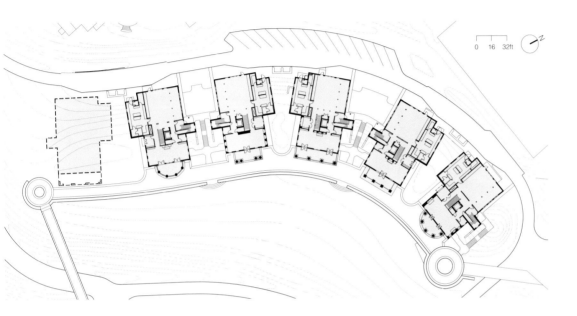

0   16   32ft

Colors and symbols were designed into each house to customize the standard plan. Stylistic cues were taken from Jeffersonian examples and late-18th and early-19th century pattern books, including period Chinese influences used in the houses' Great Hall panels and as pagoda forms over the front entries.

The houses are divided into three floors: public, semi-public, and private. The public floor has an entrance off the promenade and opens into a grand stair hall off which are located the lounge and a house-mother's apartment. The second floor contains the formal living room, dining room (for 80 women), and kitchen. The third floor contains sleeping quarters and bathrooms for 20 women.

7

155

HARVARD UNIVERSITY CAMPUS PLANNING
Cambridge, Massachusetts

The current Harvard University campus
plan is the result of a careful and strategic
planning effort, which began with its
founding in the 1680's. Over time each
college within the university assumed its
own unique identity. Open greens or
"yards" are defined by the grouping of
buildings with walking paths connecting
different precincts of the campus.

In 1977, our firm began its work on the
Harvard campus with the design of the
Sherman Fairchild Biochemistry Laboratory. One of the strongest attributes of this
laboratory's design is the creation of an
open space among the dense buildings
that surround it. Since then we have contributed to the ongoing plan for the general
university campus, the Harvard Medical
School campus, and that of Harvard's
School of Public Health.

A consistent theme throughout this work
has been the role of campus space, both
interior and exterior. Our project work—
both renovations and new buildings—has
been guided by our studies of the campus
and the Harvard community and by analy-
sis of sector plans. We have also worked
extensively with Renzo Piano on the
addition to the Fogg Art Museum and the
renovation of the Sackler Art Museum.

1 F.X.B. BUILDING
2 BUILDING 2, RENOVATION
3 SCHOOL OF DENTAL MEDICINE
4 HARVARD MEDICAL SCHOOL

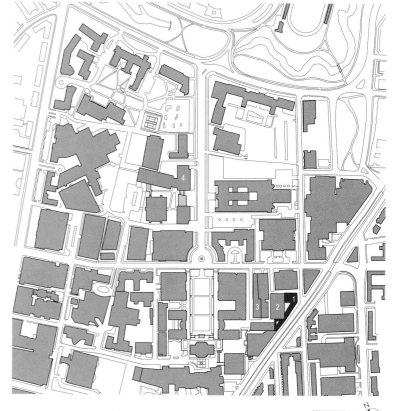

Harvard Medical School Campus in Boston

0   128   256ft

Harvard University Campus in Cambridge

0   128   256ft

N

■ BUILT PROJECT
■ PLANNED PROJECT

1 MAXWELL DWORKIN LABORATORY
2 PIERCE HALL
3 THE LINK BUILDING
4 SHERMAN FAIRCHILD BIOCHEMISTRY LABORATORY
5 THE UNIVERSITY MUSEUM OF CULTURAL & NATURAL HISTORY
6 BIOLOGICAL LABORATORY AND HERBARIUM
7 SACKLER MUSEUM
8 FOGG ART MUSEUM

Harvard University, America's first college, consists of shifting **precincts and yards**

HARVARD UNIVERSITY I MAXWELL DWORKIN LABORATORY
Cambridge, Massachusetts

1

Harvard's departments of Computer Science and Electrical Engineering required a new and larger facility to consolidate the teaching and research activities of its existing faculty and eight new appointments. Located on the western edge of Harvard's science precinct, the new building accommodates the shift from the faculty's theoretical study to experimental and systems work.

The building includes nearly 100,000 square feet of new academic space on an extremely constrained site. Since a high-rise structure was not possible, the resulting floor plates extend nearly to the edges of the available building area.

In order to mitigate the structure's mass, the design solution divides the building into manageable parts that respond to two distinct site conditions and articulate the spatial organization. A brick exterior wall wraps the building to the north and complements the traditional structures on the adjacent Law School quad. Facing the street edge, a lighter, more transparent facade of glass curtain wall and aluminum sunscreens celebrates the role of technology and discovery within the new building. The design also extends the boundary of the engineering precinct to the north while reinforcing the continuity between campus spaces to the east and west.

1   MAXWELL DWORKIN LABORATORY
2   PIERCE HALL
3   LAW SCHOOL QUAD
4   HAUSER HALL
5   HARKNESS COMMONS

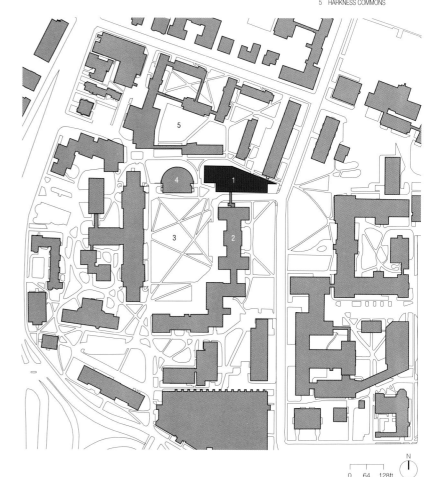

0   64   128ft

N

2

An edge building establishes a **new identity** for the quad.

3

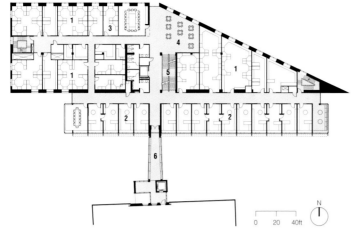

Typical Upper Floor

1 RESEARCH LAB
2 OFFICE
3 SEMINAR / CONFERENCE
4 STUDENT LOUNGE
5 COMMUNICATING STAIR
6 BRIDGE TO PIERCE HALL

N

0   20   40ft

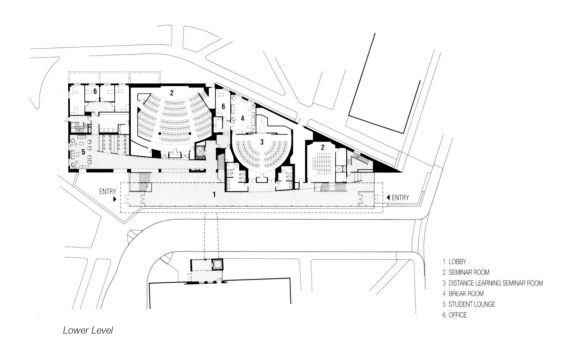

Lower Level

1 LOBBY
2 SEMINAR ROOM
3 DISTANCE LEARNING SEMINAR ROOM
4 BREAK ROOM
5 STUDENT LOUNGE
6 OFFICE

A **hierarchical** organization stratifies a complex program.

The ground-floor classrooms are connected by a linear lobby on the south side of the building. The upper floors—containing labs interspersed with offices for faculty, post-doctoral researchers, and graduate students—are linked by an open and translucent stairway at the building's center.

4

5

6

7

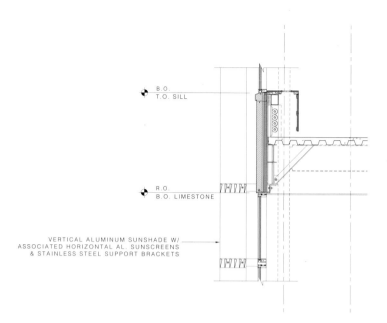

B.O.
T.O. SILL

R.O.
B.O. LIMESTONE

VERTICAL ALUMINUM SUNSHADE W/
ASSOCIATED HORIZONTAL AL. SUNSCREENS
& STAINLESS STEEL SUPPORT BRACKETS

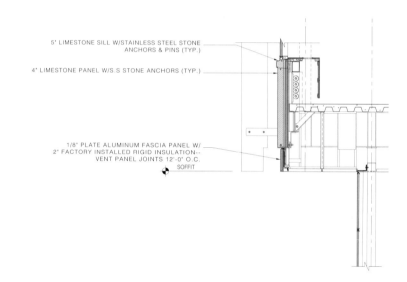

5" LIMESTONE SILL W/STAINLESS STEEL STONE
ANCHORS & PINS (TYP.)

4" LIMESTONE PANEL W/S.S STONE ANCHORS (TYP.)

1/8" PLATE ALUMINUM FASCIA PANEL W/
2" FACTORY INSTALLED RIGID INSULATION--
VENT PANEL JOINTS 12'-0" O.C.
SOFFIT

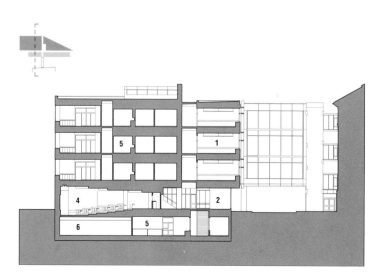

1 OFFICE
2 LOBBY
3 COMMUNICATING STAIR
4 SEMINAR/CONFERENCE/LOUNGE
5 RESEARCH LAB
6 SUPPORT

The translucent scissor stair, combined with generous open lounges, promotes interaction between disciplines and increases the opportunities for serendipitous exchanges—a crucial part of the research and learning process.

8

9

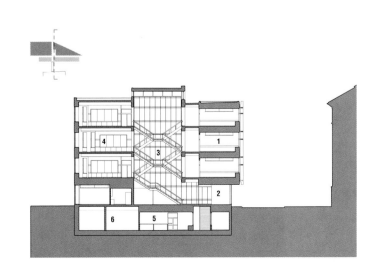

CAMBRIDGE HOSPITAL I R.E.A.C.H. PROJECT
Cambridge, Massachusetts

The Cambridge Health Alliance, dedicated to community health, is a unique
model that integrates public health, clinical care, training, and research. Cambridge Hospital, the core facility of the
alliance, was a traditional city inpatient
hospital with its last major update in the
1970s. The growth in programs for ambulatory care, teaching and research, out-
reach to community health, and the need
to integrate these programs into an expanded community network were a mis-
match with the existing infrastructure.

The Renewal and Expansion As a Center
for Community Health (R.E.A.C.H.) shifts
the focus of the hospital's program from
inpatient care and diagnostics to one
more fully centered on ambulatory and
emergency service.

The scope of work includes a new wing
for all ambulatory services, a new emergency department, and a new main entrance with a completely new campus
landscape. A new addition to the inpatient
tower connects two isolated wings, allowing staffing flexibility and additional beds.
Parking problems were solved with a four-
story underground structure.

1   AMBULATORY CARE ADDITION
2   RENOVATION
3   NEW MAIN ENTRANCE
4   SERVICE ENTRY
5   GARAGE ENTRY

0   32 64ft

A playful and reinvigorated entry addresses a multicultural **community** setting.

164

2

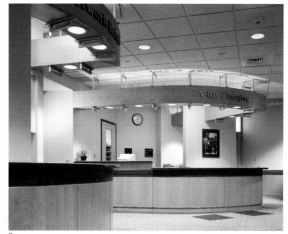

3

create patterns of space and circulation that transform its

A new circulation spine along the exterior front of the building orients patients and expresses the hospital's openness to the community. The transparency of the experience (from waiting room, to corridor, to arrival, to neighborhood) provides clarity to way-finding. Natural light and the extensive use of wood and earth tones for interior finishes help to create a warm and inviting environment.

Set within the heart of a residential neighborhood, the existing seven-story building towers over the surrounding one-, two-, and three-family wood-frame houses. In contrast to this dark brick monolith, the new addition steps down in scale to meet the height of the residential streetscape. Shifting planes and bay windows create a rhythmic pattern in scale with the adjacent buildings. A trellis and canopies at the main entrance further mediate the building's scale and detailing to the pedestrian, with references to the wooden entry porches of nearby houses.

1 MAIN DROP OFF
2 GARAGE ENTRY
3 LOBBY & PUBLIC SPINE
4 ER—WAITING
5 OUTPATIENT CLINICS

0   16   32ft

N

Entry Level

purpose or use is the building for, and how **A faceted circulation spine** reorganizes the floor plate.

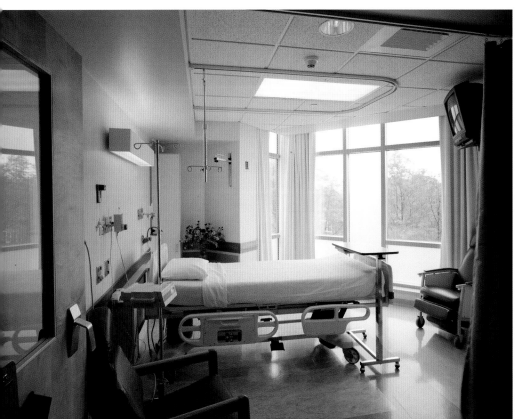

4

5

6

VETERANS AFFAIRS MEDICAL CENTER I AMBULATORY CARE ADDITION
Boston, Massachusetts

The existing Medical Center, a 14-story white metal-panel-clad tower, was built in the 1950s adjacent to Boston's Frederick Law Olmsted-designed Emerald Necklace and a low-scale neighborhood of primarily residential brick buildings. Scattered institutional buildings have brick perimeter walls that also face the main street edge. The design solution reorders the entire campus by placing the addition along the primary street wall and improving pedestrian and vehicular access. A new turnaround/drop-off/pick-up area is now located centrally among the four major buildings of the complex with the medical center tower to the upper left of the site, a new parking deck on the upper right, a hostel on the lower right, and the new ambulatory care building on the lower left of the site. The turnaround is the intersection of two tree-lined axes, which provides a new visual order to the campus.

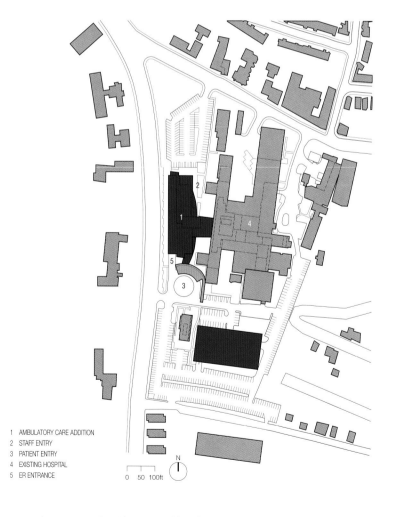

1 AMBULATORY CARE ADDITION
2 STAFF ENTRY
3 PATIENT ENTRY
4 EXISTING HOSPITAL
5 ER ENTRANCE

0 50 100ft

N

A **new urban** edge spans two entrances to the medical center.

2

3

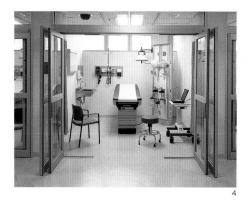

4

This project represents a new model for patient care delivery that is a dramatic change from existing ambulatory care practices in patient comfort, staff efficiency, and teaching. Ambulatory care spaces are organized into clinical modules and pods.

An illuminated canopy leads the patient from the reception desk in the lobby waiting area into the clinical modules. Each module is composed of examination rooms, consultation rooms, and administrative and clinical support spaces shared by a group of physicians. An examination pod has two exam areas, two office/ examination rooms, a toilet, and a utility room. This layout improves patient privacy and optimizes the nursing care, while accommodating teaching and training.

A band of reddish cast stone is used along the lower floors of the major street facade, anchoring the elevation at the pedestrian scale. The top floor and entrance canopy utilize light blue metal panels to create a bridge to the existing medical center tower.

1 MAIN ENTRY
2 LOWER LOBBY
3 EMERGENCY DEPARTMENT
4 COURTYARD
5 EXISTING BUILDING

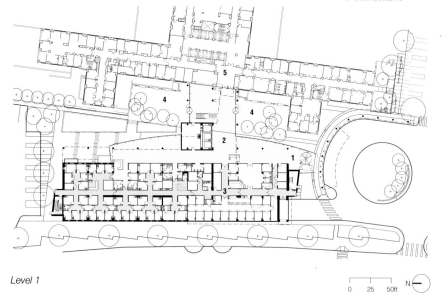

Level 1

0 25 50ft   N

5

6

Soffits and color mark the **transition** between public and private spaces.

7

BROWN UNIVERSITY
BARUS AND HOLLEY ADDITION AND RENOVATION
Providence, Rhode Island

1

In 1998, Brown University embarked on a mission to expand and unify the facilities of its Department of Engineering. An 18,000-square-foot infill pavilion accomplishes this goal and more. The addition forms a new "front door" that increases departmental visibility and becomes a key transitional space, simplifying circulation and handi-capped accessibility. In addition, it creates a formal link to Brown's main campus, acting as an extension of the school's primary pedestrian thoroughfare, Manning Walk, that passes through various pre-cincts and under several historic cere-monial arches to terminate at Barus and Holley.

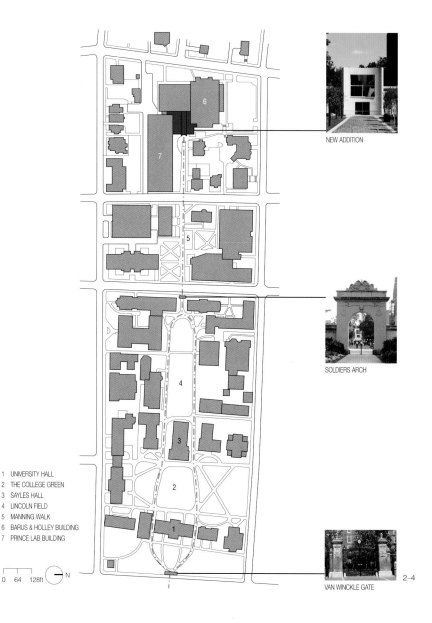

NEW ADDITION

SOLDIERS ARCH

1   UNIVERSITY HALL
2   THE COLLEGE GREEN
3   SAYLES HALL
4   LINCOLN FIELD
5   MANNING WALK
6   BARUS & HOLLEY BUILDING
7   PRINCE LAB BUILDING

0   64   128ft   N

VAN WINCKLE GATE

2–4

The addition reestablishes the main campus axis with a new **front door** for engineering.

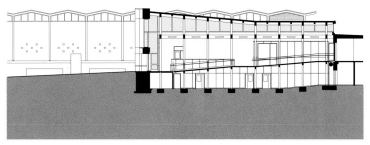

Longitudinal Section

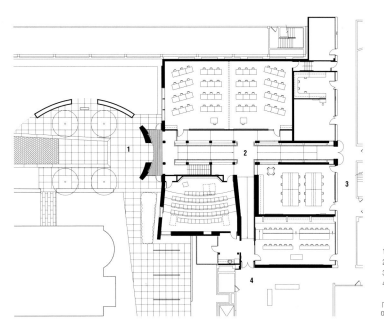

1 ENTRY PLAZA
2 RAMP SYSTEM
3 EXISTING CIRCULATION
4 EXISTING MAIN LOBBY

0   8   16ft

N

Level 1

Entered through a curved limestone archway, the pavilion is bisected by a long ramp that organizes the building. Its gentle slope, hovering in the central concourse, mitigates the varying floor elevations between adjacent buildings and resolves a 10-foot grade difference between the Engineering complex, an existing parking lot, and Manning Walk. The pavilion adds a 50-person computing room, a seminar lecture hall, and an electronics lab, all of which can be viewed from the circulation spine to demonstrate "engineering in action." High clerestory windows, vertical slotted openings at a lower level in the wall, and internal skylights flood the double-height space and working areas with natural light. A delicately inflected roof opens toward the campus, pushing the eye back out to the landscape.

A system of ramps facilitates **connections** at four different levels in three different buildi

5

life of the building, inside and out.

6

7

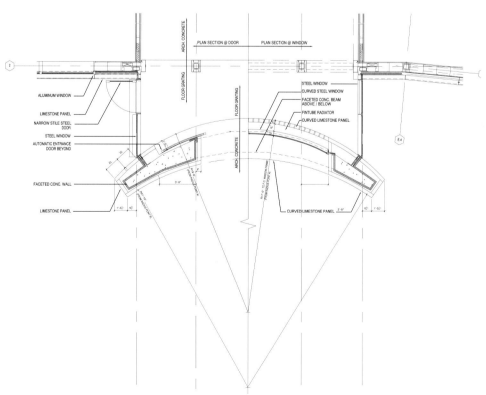

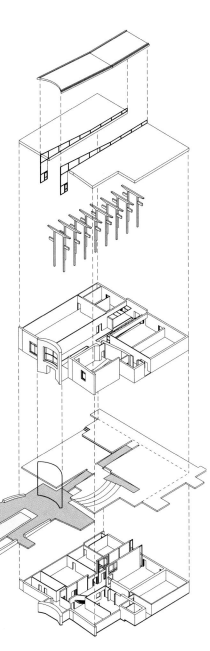

9

Prior to the addition, Manning Walk ended as a blank brick wall at the unappealing side of one Engineering building. Now, it is drawn uninterrupted across the threshold of the complex, blurring lines between interior and exterior, and linking Engineering with the larger campus. A new plaza with inviting seating and plantings further insures the building's interaction with the greater campus community. On any given class day, hundreds of people use the newly formed outdoor spaces and circulate with ease between lobbies, labs, and lecture halls.

10

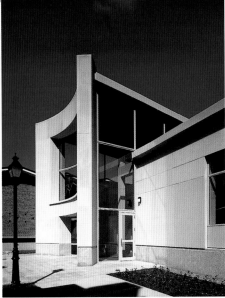

11

177

UNIVERSITY OF IOWA
MEDICAL EDUCATION AND BIOMEDICAL RESEARCH FACILITY

Iowa City, Iowa

1

The Medical Education and Biomedical Research Facility (MEBRF) is the first phase of a master plan for the Health Sciences campus at the University of Iowa. The far-reaching goal of the plan is to establish an academic campus for the pursuit of excellence in education and research. Education is envisioned as the cohesive activity on the new campus, one that brings all the Health Sciences Schools and Colleges together along a main east-west pedestrian axis.

MEBRF, completed in January 2003, houses two programs. First, it functions as the new flagship for the University's Carver College of Medicine and is home to most of its educational, student, and administration spaces. Second, MEBRF provides state-of-the-art lab space for biomedical research. All the building's users come together in a communal four-story atrium, which includes a cafe and a 250-seat auditorium.

The atrium is located at the south end of the building at the confluence of two major campus pathways and several other Health Sciences buildings. It has become the social and academic center on campus. Its geometry accommodates the major pathway to the hospital, complemented by an open stair along the same axis. The auditorium is articulated as a large copper volume, providing a backdrop for the cafe and the lower atrium.

1 MEDICAL EDUCATION AND BIOMEDICAL RESEARCH FACILI
2 ATRIUM
3 MEDICAL EDUCATION AND RESEARCH BUILDING
4 HEALTH SCIENCES BUILDING
5 NEWTON RD. PARKING FACILIT

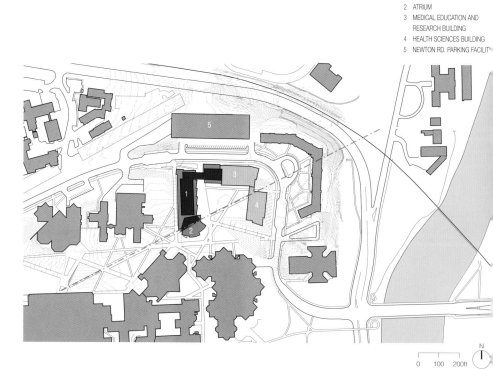

0   100   200ft

N

The first **component** of a new quad for the sciences.

2

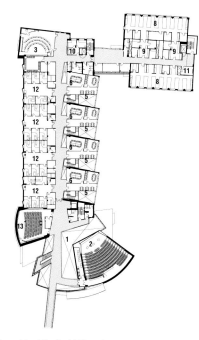

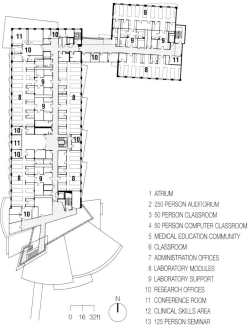

Level 1 - Medical Education　　　　*Level 2 - Medical Education*　　　　*Levels 3,4 - Research*

1 ATRIUM
2 250 PERSON AUDITORIUM
3 50 PERSON CLASSROOM
4 50 PERSON COMPUTER CLASSROOM
5 MEDICAL EDUCATION COMMUNITY
6 CLASSROOM
7 ADMINISTRATION OFFICES
8 LABORATORY MODULES
9 LABORATORY SUPPORT
10 RESEARCH OFFICES
11 CONFERENCE ROOM
12 CLINICAL SKILLS AREA
13 125 PERSON SEMINAR

0 16 32ft

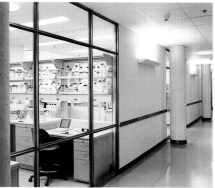

4

purpose or use is the building

5

6

Teaching communities are expressed in the building form and geometry.

The design team was fortunate to work with the College of Medicine as a new medical curriculum was designed. The resulting spaces are architecturally innovative in the way they provide an environment matched to the needs of medical education. For example, the cluster of four "student communities" takes the form of two-story spaces facing the central corridor on the west side and the quadrangle on the east. Each cluster includes open and private study space, social area, a classroom, and student support offices to provide the academic and social infrastructure of student life. Clinical skills suites provide a setting where students are trained with the use of simulated patients.

7

8

9

The exterior of MEBRF reflects its diverse
inner life. The repetitive and disciplined
lab modules with identical windows on the
upper floors are clad in local limestone. In
contrast, spaces for the medical education program on the lower floors possess a
sculptural variety, and are clad in weathered copper panels. Ample use of glass
creates the sense of openness, both
inside the building and to the landscape
beyond. The landscape is designed as a
continuous environment with the building,
enforcing its connections with the Health
Sciences campus.

10

OBERLIN COLLEGE I NEW SCIENCE CENTER
Oberlin, Ohio

Designed expressly for contemporary
teaching methods, this new Science
Center enables Oberlin College to retain
its national position as a premier educator
of future scientists and also allows the
departments of biology, chemistry, neuroscience, and physics, and a vastly enlarged science library, to be housed in
one central location on campus.

Oberlin's existing science facility, the
1960s Kettering Science Building, created
a 330-foot-long barrier ("The Great Wall of
Science") along a heavily traveled vehicular and pedestrian street (West
Lorain), essentially cutting off the rest of
the campus. This separation of the sciences from the surrounding campus
created both a physical and intellectual
schism. The design team took to heart
Oberlin's programmatic, space, and
image problems and created a campus
plan that comprises 150,000 square feet
of new construction and 80,000 square
feet of renovation.

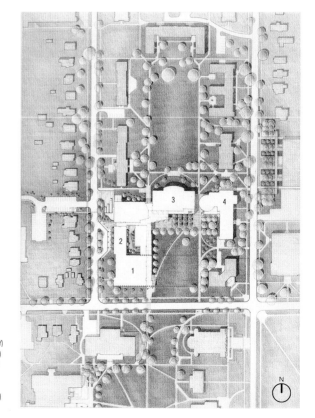

1   KETTERING BUILDING (BIOLOGY)
    (ORIGINAL FOOTPRINT DOTTED)
2   WEST WING SPERRY BUILDING
    (BIOLOGICAL SCIENCES)
3   NORTH WING
    (CHEMISTRY/SCIENCE LIBRARY)
4   WRIGHT BUILDING (PHYSICS)

The project extends the primary academic **quad** to include all the sciences.

184

The focus for both client and designers was to repair the existing science department fragmentation, support a more holistic approach linking diverse science disciplines, and create a stronger image for the sciences on campus. This project is unique in that the new building establishes a strong science presence in a primarily arts-based community. Located at the heart of Oberlin's residential and academic quadrangle (with classical Cass Gilbert college buildings nearby), the new facility reinforces dominant campus use patterns by extending existing pathways through and around the campus with little interruption.

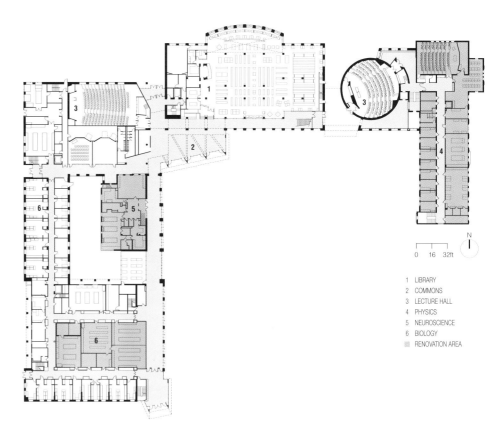

0   16   32ft

N

1   LIBRARY
2   COMMONS
3   LECTURE HALL
4   PHYSICS
5   NEUROSCIENCE
6   BIOLOGY
▨   RENOVATION AREA

2

3

Disciplines are arranged in a **wave** of interdisciplinary adjacencies.

4

5

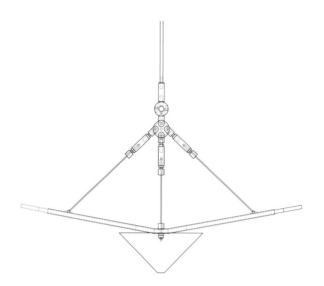

Detail of Light Fixture in Commons

9

In keeping with modern pedagogical methods, the Center's architecture blurs the distinction between the disciplines, allowing for growth and large-scale flexibility, while also melding some of Oberlin's more storied campus landmarks into its design. Internally, disciplines are arranged from left to right in a "wave" of interdisciplinary adjacencies that share related utility infrastructures. These blurred boundaries allow for the growth of one department into another, and flexibility for spontaneous collaboration across specialties.

10

WEST VIRGINIA UNIVERSITY | LIFE SCIENCES BUILDING
Morgantown, West Virginia

At 200,000 square feet, the West Virginia University Life Sciences Building (LSB) contains interdisciplinary research and undergraduate classrooms for the sciences. The largest building on campus, it serves more than 4,000 people during peak hours. This project is the first in a long-range master plan for the Lower Bowl area, which includes future projects for a Forensic Science Building and a parking garage.

Recalling the scale of industrial buildings along Morgantown's waterfront, the LSB works to define a new horizon for the campus. The steeply sloped site is oriented towards the Monongahela River; its grade is more than three stories below the main campus level.

Sited to reinforce and improve the definition of a new quadrangle for the Lower Bowl, the LSB is visibly open and accessible from all grade levels abutting it, with seven grade-level entrances and four lobbies. These elements are spread across a changing building section that adapts at each entrance to reduce the scale of the building as it meets the grade.

1 LIFE SCIENCES BUILDING
2 FUTURE FORENSIC SCIENCE
3 FUTURE BUILDING
4 FUTURE PARKING
5 HISTORIC WOODBARN CIRCLE
6 LOWER BOWL

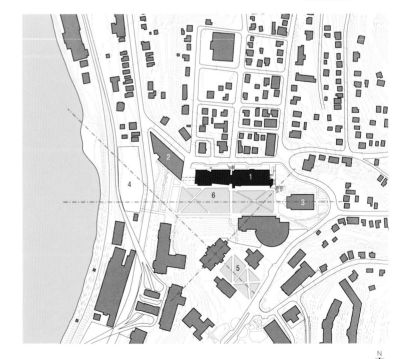

0   100 200ft

A megastructure woven into a steeply slopping site defines a new **horizon** for the campus

190

2

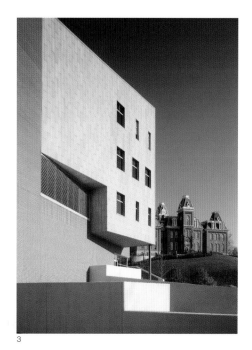

3

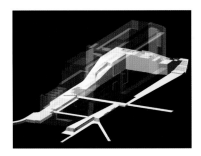

Ground Plane

Levels 4,5 - Biology Research Labs

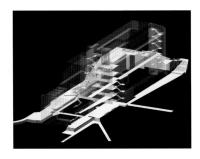

Circulation

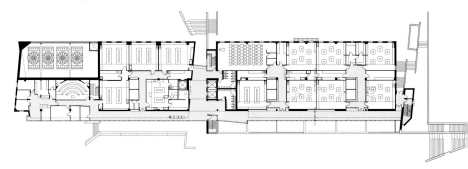

Level 3 - Biology Teaching Labs

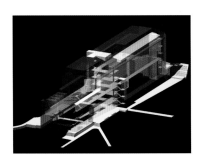

Envelope

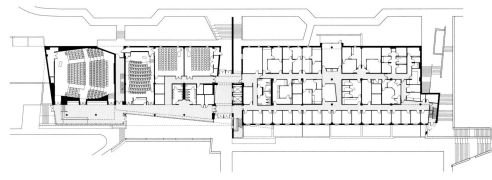

Lower Level, Level 1 - General Classrooms, Psychology Research

hat purpose or use is the building for, and how do its program and parti shape it? How are these activities int

The LSB consolidates the departments of biology and psychology into one integrated facility. Most of the building is dedicated to research and teaching labs, with the ground floor dedicated to general-purpose classrooms shared by the entire university. An 8,000-square-foot greenhouse occupies the roof, while a shared 6,000-square-foot animal facility is in the basement.

The south facade reveals the programmatic layering of the building with two floors of psychology defined by a brick podium and three floors of biology by a glass curtain wall system.

5

6

7

A **layered massing** strategy expresses program and human occupancy.

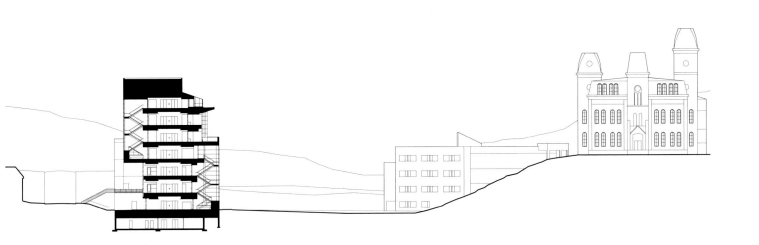

8

Defining a new north edge to the downtown campus, the LSB negotiates a transition between a formal, ceremonial quad to the south and a low-scale residential area to the north. Reflecting this dichotomy, the two main facades switch the relationship of wall to void, break the volume to soften the articulation on the street side, and formalize the quad face with a roof canopy. Both end facades express the overlapping of these systems.

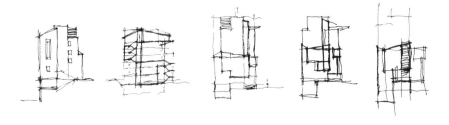

The exterior materials reflect the dual need to respect the traditions of the local academic architecture while projecting an image of state-of-the-art science for the first major science facility on campus in over 40 years. Brick, copper, and glass form the primary exterior palette. These materials are combined in different ways to address a range of formal concerns that explore varying degrees of transparency and solidity on each facade.

Changes in material also address orientation, changes in program, and help formalize scale relationships with the more typical three-story scale of the surrounding campus buildings.

9

10

11

LOOKING AHEAD

JOHNS HOPKINS UNIVERSITY
SCHOOL OF MEDICINE I BROADWAY RESEARCH BUILDING

Baltimore, Maryland

1

The Broadway Research Building (BRB) is a 371,900-square-foot medical research-facility sited at the corner of North Broadway and East Madison Street. Conceived to define the northwest corner of the campus and to provide identity to an otherwise rambling ensemble of urban research facilities, the BRB houses research laboratories, lab support spaces, a vivarium, and the administrative offices for the medical school.

Urbanistically, the building adheres to the geometry of the city, with the long rectangular volume establishing the streetscape to the north and west. The setback from the adjacent buildings to the south creates a new campus space internal to the block. Starting at the east end, the building volume steps back to the west to accommodate the vehicular drop-off. This establishes a gateway opening to campus from Broadway, the main north-south axis. The BRB provides the new front door to the medical school.

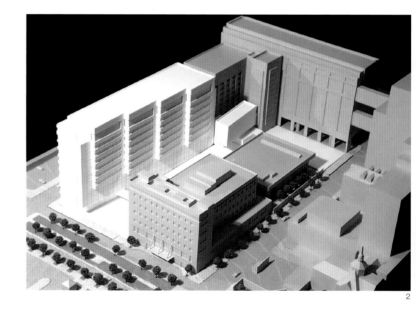

2

A new pavilion and courtyard are created to **unify** a research precinct.

Internally, the plan is layered with open laboratories to the north, an interior support core, and researcher offices to the south. The stepped form along the south wall creates clusters of offices that form research neighborhoods, and expands views to downtown Baltimore.

Three elements, conceived as parallelograms, enhance the composition and symbolically address issues of presence, identity, and connection. These parallelograms alternately complement, collide with, or set the limits of the main volume: a. The tilted ground plane defines the structured courtyard, detached from the ground plane; b. The pavilion at the focal point of the courtyard forms a symbolic gathering space, floating among the structures at the center of the block and connecting the new building internally to the campus; c. The blade slices through the stepped volume of the main building, connecting the arrival to the heart of campus and forming the public path that organizes the access to the administrative programs.

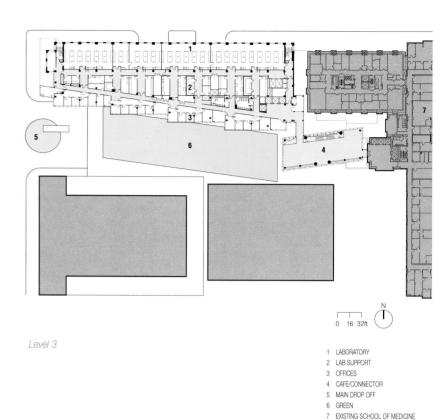

Level 3

0 16 32ft

N

1 LABORATORY
2 LAB SUPPORT
3 OFFICES
4 CAFE/CONNECTOR
5 MAIN DROP OFF
6 GREEN
7 EXISTING SCHOOL OF MEDICINE

3

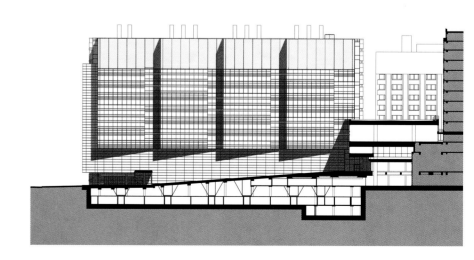

Elaborate curtainwall and precast wall systems express a **dynamic** building form.

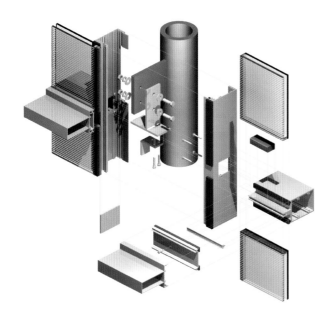

5

4

PENNSYLVANIA STATE UNIVERSITY
CHEMISTRY AND LIFE SCIENCES BUILDINGS

University Park, Pennsylvania

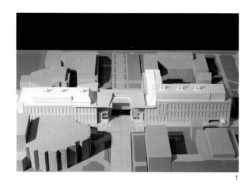

This complex is a rich combination of classrooms and research laboratories that initially began as two separate commissions and eventually grew together. Linked by an above-grade connection that forms a "gateway to the sciences," the combined buildings enhance the culture of interdisciplinary research. The gateway houses a range of common meeting spaces for formal and informal gatherings and is the centerpiece of the organization behind the 330,000-square-foot complex.

The buildings shape a wide array of campus spaces. The gateway is sited at the head of a new pedestrian mall between the two buildings. A piazza connecting with the performing arts complex to the north of the gateway defines the entry portal to the core campus. Each building defines its own unique courtyard. The Chemistry courtyard is intimate, containing two existing cottages and a specimen elm tree. The Life Sciences courtyard is much more public, defined by several levels of student seating and gathering areas to handle the bustling undergraduate classroom activity on the ground floor.

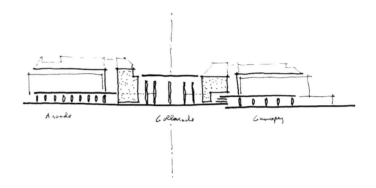

1   LIFE SCIENCES BUILDING
2   CHEMISTRY RESEARCH BUILDING
3   GATEWAY
4   CHEMISTRY COURTYARD
5   LSB COURTYARD
6   SHORTLIDGE MALL
7   PIAZZA
8   FUTURE QUADRANGLE

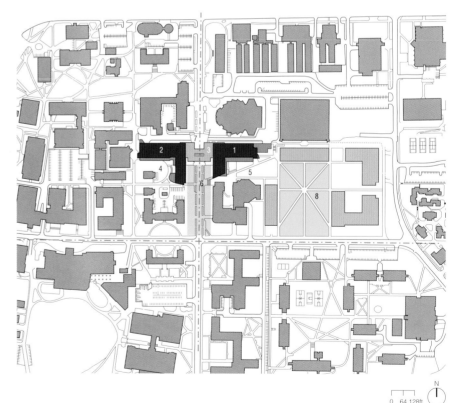

0   64 128ft

Four distinct **outdoor rooms** were defined to create a new science precinct.

2

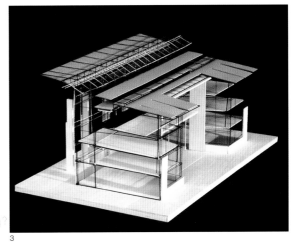

patterns of space and circulation that transform its setting?   prese

3

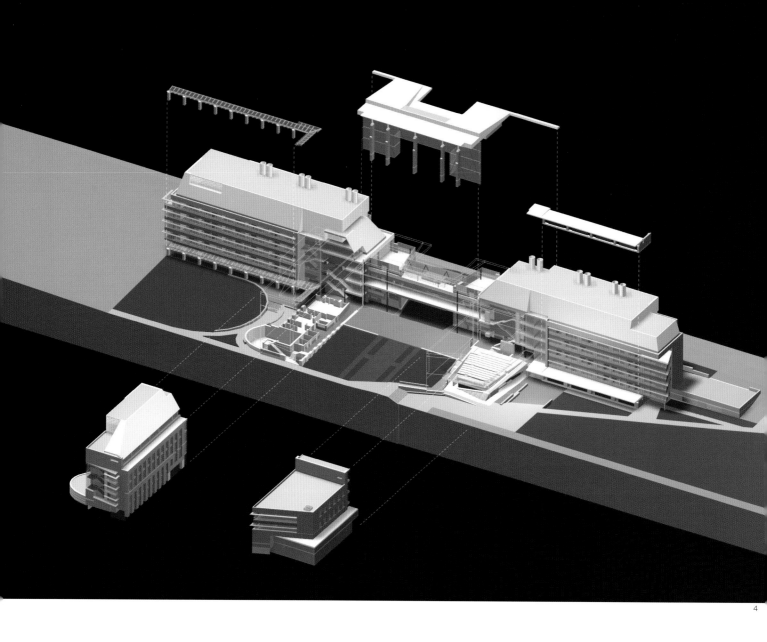

4

The plan is organized around a glass spine that flows in the east-west direction, connecting the buildings. This spine organizes both the inside and outside spaces with a grade-level arcade along the courtyard of the Chemistry Building that extends into the monumental colonnade at the head of the Shortlidge Mall and into the Life Sciences Building. On the inside, the spine takes the shape of a single corridor laced with an intricate network of communicating stairs, the two-story gateway at the center, and lounges at the ends.

Brick pavilions facing the Shortlidge Mall define the formal facades of the building, while a more informal curtain wall assembly defines the courtyard spaces, revealing the sciences. By making reference to the architecture of the sciences from the earlier part of the 20th century at Penn State, two-floor masonry openings are consistently used for the laboratory spaces, yet the composition and massing of each facade is slightly different as a response to the program and site forces unique to each location.

5

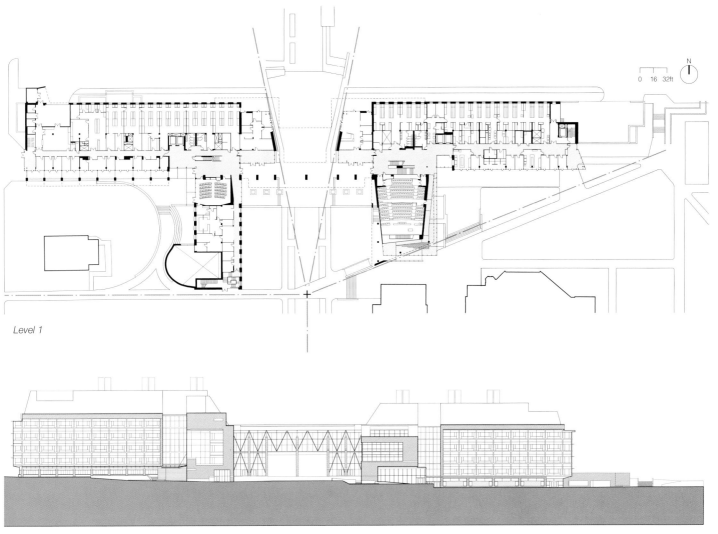

Level 1

South Elevation

Science mega-structure contains multiple planning prototypes.

6

An occupied **bridge connection** allows programs to cross-pollinate.

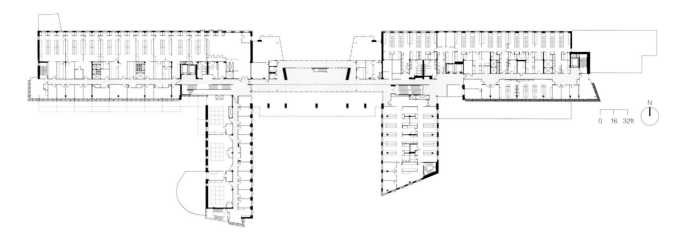

Level 3

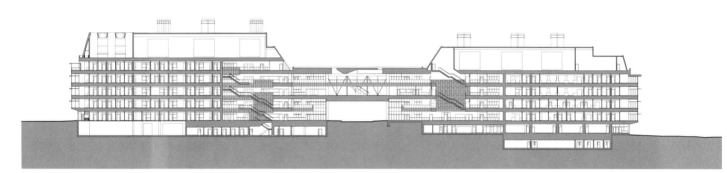

Section

Numerous programs and lab typologies define an extremely flexible lab culture. The Life Sciences Building contains four themes: animal research, neurosciences, toxicology, and plant research. It also has a faculty commons, student commons, general-purpose classrooms, and a 250-seat auditorium. The Chemistry Building contains research space for synthetic chemistry, biochemistry, instrumentation, mass spectroscopy, a large NMR facility, and departmental seminar and conference functions.

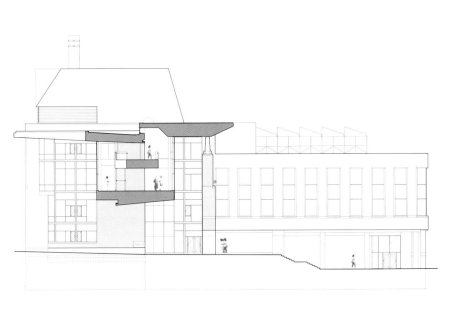

THE ROCKEFELLER UNIVERSITY | NEW RESEARCH BUILDING

New York, New York

As a prestigious research institution in the heart of New York City, The Rockefeller University is faced with a number of unique challenges to its growth. The continued success of the institution is clearly tied to its ability to lure and keep some of the world's most highly esteemed researchers. Beyond the richness of its scientific community, Rockefeller strives to maintain an attractive environment through the development of state-of-the-art, progressive laboratories set in a unique, spectacular urban setting.

The University is located along the East River, centered on 66th Street. An oasis within the fabric of the city, the campus has the second largest green space in Manhattan. Its tree-lined paths and carefully maintained plantings have become an essential element in the identity of the University.

1　NEW RESEARCH BUILDING
2　RENOVATION
3　FIT OUT OF FLOORS 10,11,12
4　FUTURE BUILDING SITE

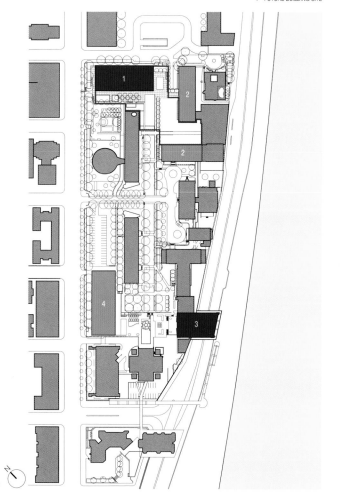

0 64 128ft

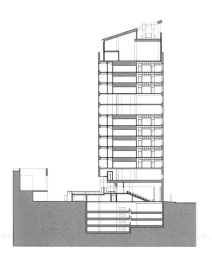

A high-tech **landmark** building on a historic landmark site.

208

*A suspended lighting cloud and shelving system allow for a fully **flexible** laboratory bench.*

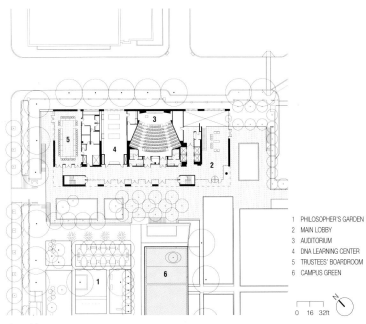

1 PHILOSOPHER'S GARDEN
2 MAIN LOBBY
3 AUDITORIUM
4 DNA LEARNING CENTER
5 TRUSTEES' BOARDROOM
6 CAMPUS GREEN

0 16 32ft

N

Level 1

Formally, the building emulates some of the original Rockefeller laboratory buildings. Proportions and window patterns have been designed to fit within the language of the existing architecture. The building's materials reflect some of the campus' more recent structures. The dark gray granite base, buff-colored terra cotta tile body, silvery gray curtain wall and corners, red metal roof, and Indiana limestone accents near the entry tie the building to its immediate urban context.

The typical laboratory floor plan is based on a veneered planning approach developed in response to specific comments and needs of the Rockefeller scientists. The design and construction of this building will be part of a long-term master plan, designed by our firm, to upgrade many of the research buildings on campus. In addition to providing larger spaces for growing laboratories, it offers swing space to be used during the renovation of other existing laboratories and updating of the complete campus infrastructure.

The landscape at The Rockefeller University is an integral part of the institution. It is intertwined with the University's history and serves several roles within campus life. This relationship to the context is critical in how the New Research Building (NRB) relates to the prominent landscape features of the campus. At ground level, the building provides a large lobby as an extension of the campus green. The Philosopher's Garden is the building's most important neighbor. Designed by Dan Kiley, the garden's appeal lies in the intimate spaces created by the formal arrangement of lush plantings and garden elements. The NRB has been sited specifically not to overpower the garden but to share in its beauty. A large trustee meeting room overlooks the garden.

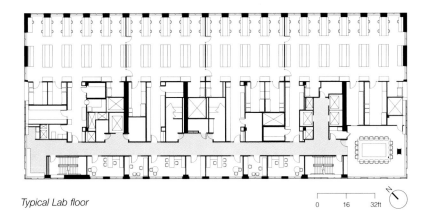

Typical Lab floor

0   16   32ft

3

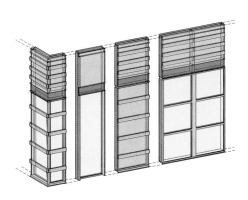

The exterior of the building will be clad with a prefabricated module system composed of terra cotta, metal panel, and glass.

PRINCETON UNIVERSITY | GUYOT HALL ADDITION

Princeton, New Jersey

1

Guyot Hall, one of the earliest buildings in the U.S. constructed expressly for science education, has been home to Princeton University's departments of biology and geology since 1909. The Collegiate Gothic structure has been modified and added to many times as the departments have evolved over the past century. Responding to recent developments in the earth sciences (increased faculty research, undergraduate interest, and interdisciplinary consolidation), a new addition to Guyot establishes a science complex. The addition includes 150,000 square feet of new construction interconnected to the Guyot Hall science complex, plus 30,000 square feet of renovations.

1   GUYOT RENOVATION
2   GUYOT ADDITION
3   SCHULTZ LABORATORY
4   MOFFETT LABORATORY

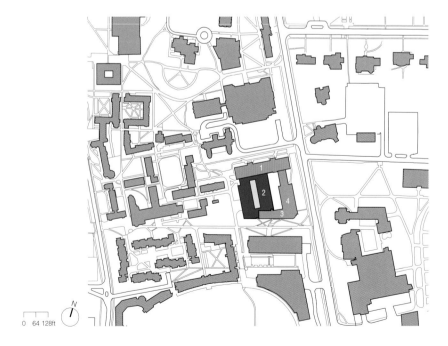

0   64   128ft

The addition **mediates** between the Collegiate Gothic Guyot Hall and Post Modern Schultz Lab.

The new construction is placed between Collegiate Gothic Guyot Hall and the Schultz Laboratory, designed by our firm and Robert Venturi in 1994. The design completes the formerly open-ended complex by inserting a simple mass that blends the two structures with a focal point at the southwest corner adjacent to Schultz. The addition's terra cotta facades float above a limestone base that mediates the steep slope and reflects the base treatment of both Guyot and Shultz. Window, door, and loading-area openings are carved away to reveal the thickness and density of both the base level itself and the programmatic spaces beyond.

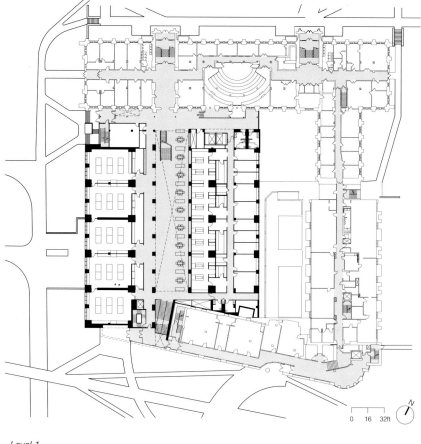

Level 1

0 16 32ft

purpose or use is the building for, and how do its program and parts shape it? How are these activities inter... Sustainable strategies including a g...

2

f and heat wheel recovery system celebrate the purpose of the building.

The addition's central multi-story concourse—the Great Room—creates a public space that organizes the new building and connects it to Guyot and to the campus beyond. In the spirit of Princeton's quadrangles, this space is conceived as a microcosm of the university at large—a public "living room" that allows spatial, programmatic, circulatory, and tectonic overlaps to occur. The warm wood panels that line the space relate rhythmically to the exterior terra cotta tiles but clearly suggest an interior space appropriate for both formal and informal gatherings.

Light plays an important role in the Guyot addition. Penetration of daylight into inhabited spaces is controlled through various layers of filters. Direct light from the south and west is filtered through screens of terra cotta "baguettes." The resulting play of light/shadow and transparency/opacity models and defines views from the lab space directly to the outside. A large skylight over the Great Room transmits soft light throughout the day. At night, uplighting illuminates the skylight from within to produce a luminous and inviting glow.

4

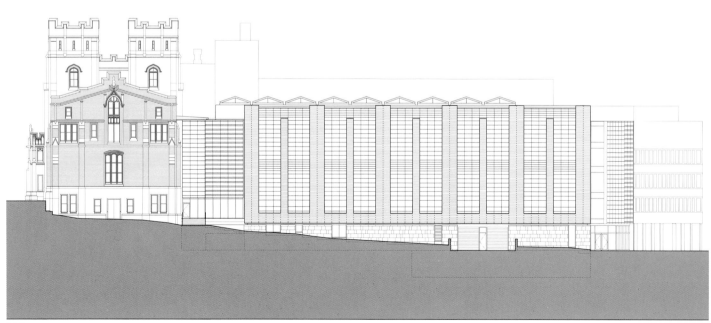

Terra cotta tile and baguette system is used for **sun screening and rain screen cladding.**

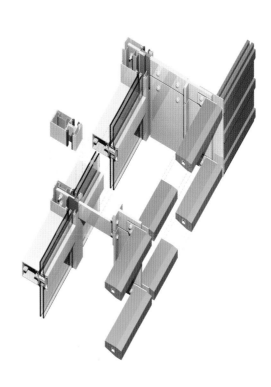

5

6

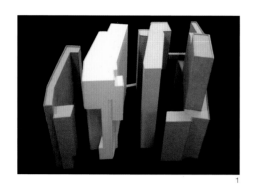

1

At 330,000 square feet, the 11-story Biomedical Sciences Tower III is one of the largest projects undertaken at the University of Pittsburgh. When completed, the building will serve as a new front door to the research community from Fifth Avenue, one of the premier urban boulevards in the city. Connected to the University's Bioscience Tower II on the sixth floor via a bridge, Tower III will have two main lobbies and entrances, a two-floor sky-lobby accessed by the bridge on level six overlooking the city, and a prominent corner entry on Fifth Avenue. The modulation of the building's twin bars of laboratories (what we refer to as the "Gemini" floor plan) both maximizes the number of laboratories within the given allowed square footage and anchors its position at the meeting point of the University's upper campus and lower campus grids, along the main corridor of the city's institutional buildings.

The building's scale is modulated by four distinct bands of materials that step up the hill. Each layer is a contingent, yet contrasting form. The first layer, the south elevation fronting Fifth Avenue, is a monumental limestone canvas of planes and textures that register changes in program or alignment through the surface of the

stone. The next three layers are a metal/glass system, a louver system, and another limestone facade facing north. While the south-facing limestone band is based on texture and relief, the north elevation is based on silhouette and profile. The side elevations, east and west, reflect the complexity of the layering system as the four adjacent structures step up the hill.

1 BST 1 & BST 2
2 SCHOOL OF NURSING
3 BST 3
4 SCAIFE HALL

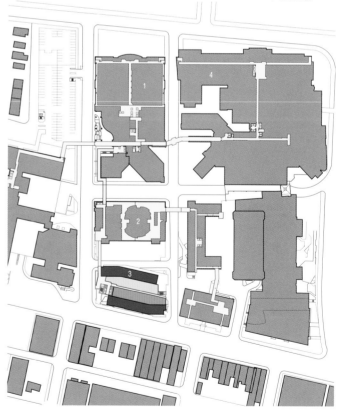

0   80   160ft

N

does the The building is composed of **four massing layers** that step up the hillside.

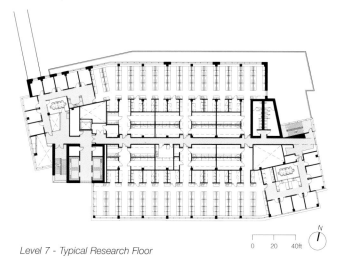

Level 7 - Typical Research Floor

0   20   40ft

N

Functionally, the building is organized into two bars of laboratory facilities, sheared by a central corridor. Within each bar, modular laboratories with support spaces run parallel and adjacent to each other, capped by office spaces at each end, east and west. These functional zones also define the layering structure for the four exterior layers. Vertical circulation cores and mechanical shafts are located on the east and west ends of the building, as are clusters of offices (which promote interaction), break areas, and conference rooms, mirroring the Gemini form of the building.

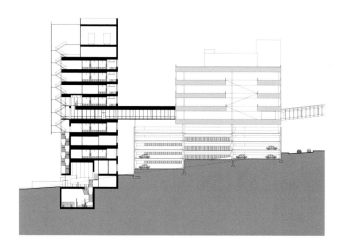

Section - Through Street Lobby & Sky Lobby

A **Gemini plan** configuration is used to shape the program spaces.

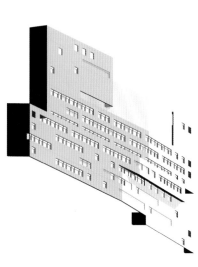

North Facade – Silhouette

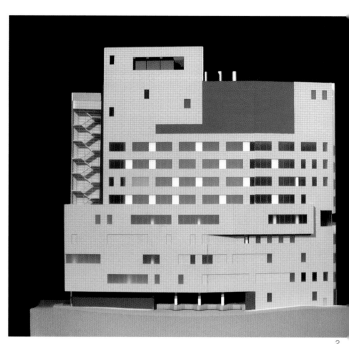

mes an **urban canvas**.

life of the building, inside and out, day

3

4

South Facade - Textured

APPENDIX

COLLABORATORS

Principals

J Ian Adamson, AIA
Ian joined Payette Associates in 1992 after practicing with firms in Philadelphia, England and Germany. He designs sophisticated college and university science, medical school, and technology facilities supporting teaching and research. His recent work has expanded to include buildings for student life. Ian's regard for context was cultivated in the eclectic environment of his previous firm, Venturi Scott Brown and Associates. Through design, he seeks to reveal the specific and local qualities of each project. A graduate of The Pennsylvania State University, where he received a Bachelor of Architecture with Distinction, Ian is a regular contributor to Project Kaleidoscope and the co-author of "Trends in Laboratory Design" for *Architectural Record Review.*

Jeffery J Burke, AIA
Since joining Payette Associates in 1979, Jeff has balanced commissions for college and university science and medical education with those for corporate biotechnology and biopharmaceutical research. His design utilizes an intensive communication process to elicit subtle distinctions of program and culture, and infuses projects with the amenities that support the recruiting and comfort of top scientists. Jeff is a graduate of Syracuse University, where he received Bachelor of Architecture and Master of Architecture degrees. He is a member of the Syracuse University School of Architecture Advisory Board. In addition, Jeff is a frequent lecturer at industry-related conferences and has taught laboratory design courses at Harvard's Graduate School of Design.

Sho-Ping Chin, AIA
First joining the firm in 1990, Sho-Ping returned in 2000 after leading her own healthcare practice for several years. She now guides Payette's healthcare team, using design to synthesize the challenges presented by rapid advances in medical technology with the real human needs of patients and caregivers. Sho-Ping works with university research hospitals, community hospitals, charitable services, and international health assistance groups. Her design is noted for its sensitivity to the psychological needs of patients, staff, and families—for comfort, clarity, simplicity, and efficiency. Sho-Ping earned her Bachelor of Arts as well as her Master of Architecture from Princeton University.

James H Collins Jr., AIA
Jim has served as President of Payette Associates since 1998, after joining the firm in 1979. He is an energetic advocate for the practice's design focus and a vital link to our clients. As a practicing architect, he designs research environments in campus settings. His design elevates the craft of building and is noted for its prototypical inventiveness. Jim is a graduate of Rensselaer Polytechnic Institute where he earned both Bachelor of Architecture and Master of Business Administration degrees with Distinction. In 2003, he was awarded the Rensselaer Alumni Association Fellows Award honoring an individual of exceptional achievement. Jim is an active lecturer and has served on numerous design juries, boards, and advisory groups for architectural education. He is the author

of "Design Process for the Human Workplace," in *The Architecture of Science*, published by MIT Press.

George E Marsh Jr., AIA
George joined Payette Associates after receiving his Bachelor of Architecture from Carnegie Mellon University. He works on a broad range of project types including healthcare, college and university research and teaching, museum, and performing arts commissions. George is known for his evocative sketches that investigate a project's spirit and rally consensus—and for the power this technique has to ignite a client's enthusiasm and inspire fundraising. George is an occasional speaker and a writer for publications such as the *New England Journal of Medicine.*

Robert F Mattox, FAIA
Bob joined Payette Associates in 1997, assuming the position of Chief Operating Officer. In this role, he oversees the firm's financial, administrative, marketing, and technological planning and brings order to the usually chaotic business of managing architectural firms. Bob has extensive experience in this task and has both taught and written on the subject. His books include *Financial Management for Architects, Standardized Accounting for Architects*, and he is co-author of *Success Strategies for Design Professionals*. He earned his Bachelor of Architecture from Rice University and his Master of Business Administration from the University of Michigan.

Thomas M Payette, FAIA, RIBA
In over 40 years as a practicing architect at Payette Associates, Tom has been at the forefront of healthcare and science design, pioneering ideas and innovations that have transformed these building typologies and molded Payette Associates into the firm it is today. Tom realized the significance of the profound human activity occurring within highly ordered buildings for health and defined a new design paradigm. In this approach, the unity of the public and private, interior and exterior, social and technical experience of place is essential. These principles are the foundation of Payette's practice to this day. Tom has realized this vision in projects throughout the United States and internationally. He has promoted this attitude in both professional and civic circles, teaching at Harvard and Rhode Island School of Design, and serving on the boards of the Boston Society of Architects, the Boston Architectural Center, the Boston Foundation for Architecture, and various AIA committees. Tom received a Bachelor of Science in Structural Engineering magna cum laude from Michigan State University and his Master of Architecture from Harvard Graduate School of Design. Tom is the author of "Ambulatory Care Facilities" in *Building Type Basics for Healthcare Facilities*, published by Wiley.

Jonathan B Romig, AIA
Jon joined Payette Associates in 1983. He designs research and teaching buildings for academic and biomedical institutions and pharmaceutical and biotechnology corporations. His work spans a breadth of scale, ranging from the design of a fume hood to the programming of a laboratory

to the master planning of a campus. Jon's work reflects a strong concern for the human and social qualities of the science environment. He has lectured for the Society for College and University Planning, Tradeline and Project Kaleidoscope. Jon is a graduate of the Rhode Island School of Design (RISD). He continues to teach at RISD and the Eagleston Institute in Sanford, ME, and to act as a National Institutes of Health grant reviewer.

Robert J Schaeffner Jr., AIA
Bob came to Payette Associates in 1981 after earning his Bachelor of Architecture from Rhode Island School of Design. His work focuses on the design of science teaching and research buildings for colleges and universities, particularly those in liberal arts settings. Coining the phrase "Sputnik-Era Science Structures" in a 1997 article in Planning for Higher Education, Bob identified the typical structural/pedagogical failures of 1960s-era science buildings. His insights have influenced new design concepts for the current surge of interdisciplinary science facility development. Bob's own design has applied these insights, resolving complicated programs in a refined and well-considered architecture that simultaneously supports vitality and interaction.

Kevin B Sullivan, AIA
Since joining Payette Associates in 1987, Kevin has designed healthcare and academic science projects, both domestically and internationally. In his work, he applies an intellectually rigorous process to address the human dimension of science projects. Kevin generates spaces and forms that are rich in color, light, and spatial depth. He received his Bachelor of Architecture magna cum laude from Virginia Polytechnic Institute and his Master of Architecture from the Harvard University Graduate School of Design. He has been honored by the Boston Society of Architects as a recipient of its Young Architect Award for design. He is a frequent studio critic at the Boston Architectural Center, the Rhode Island School of Design, and the Harvard Graduate School of Design, as well as a recurring lecturer at the Society of College and University Planners and Tradeline.

John L Wilson, FAIA
John joined Payette Associates in 1966, after receiving his Bachelor of Arts cum laude from Harvard College and a Master of Architecture from Harvard University Graduate School of Design. He has contributed significantly to healthcare design throughout the world, from rural Maine to Ethiopia, continually sharing his knowledge through publications and lectures at conferences for Tradeline, the Society for Ambulatory Care Professionals, and the American Hospital Association. He founded and co-chairs the Boston Society of Architects Task Force to End Homelessness, which assists facilities that serve the homeless population. John is a recipient of the national AIA Whitney M. Young Jr. Award, recognizing his significant professional contribution to solving pressing social issues. His AIA Fellowship was also conferred in recognition of this social focus.

Associate Principals

Christopher E Baylow, AIA
Gary J Cabo, AIA
Leon W Drachman
David G Feth, AIA
Arlen Li, AIA
Barry A Shiel, AIA

Associates

Constantine G Antoniades
Leon V Auvil, AIA
Mark D Careaga
Brian J Carlic, ASLA
Jeffrey H DeGregorio, AIA
Ginger C Desmond, AIA
Edgar M Fowler Jr., AIA
Dieter H Gartner
Matthew J Genta, AIA
Ching-Hua Ho
Jonathan R Kanda, AIA
Charles S Klee, AIA
Gary M Lepore, AIA
Scott D Parker, AIA
Robert C Pasersky
William E Riley
Agus I Rusli
Stephen W Schram
Todd C Sloane, AIA
George A Takoudes, AIA

Staff

Diego F Arango
Christopher L Baumbach
Jennifer A Bentley
Ronald F Blanchard
Pauline T Bogle
Lucretia M Bouyer
Sarah G Bowers
Virginia O Burgess
Yun-Kyung Chung
Eric G Crockwell
Heather Y DeGregorio
David J Dempsey
Marie K Denis
Brandon M Diem
Sara M Diem
Jeffery K Dumars
Christopher J Dumont
Rachel G Dumont
Yasemin A Erten
Barry R Farquharson
Jonathan D Fournier
Enno Fritsch
Mary F Gallagher
Santiago S. Garay
Elizabeth F Good

Jennifer L Hegarty
Stephanie C Hodal
William E Hoisington
Patrick A Jones
Michael R Juros
Jong-Ho Kim
Mee R Kim
Eric C Kimball
Priscilla C Klotz
Eric J Lankes
Karen D Lanoue
Eunju Lee
Seunghwan Lee
Janel L Levadoux
Michael P Liporto
Peter G Longley
Allan D Martin
Jennifer R Martinelli
Marty L McCammon
Jeffrey J Minard
Montserrat Minguell
Leocadia S Monteiro
James Morrison Jr.
Lennie L Murphy
Sarah Najmi
Michael A Norian
Deborah A O'Brien
Peter C Patsouris
Anna J Perri
Kathleen M Perry
Christina J Pungerchar
Michael J Quinn
Annie H Reed
Robert C Ritger
Sara L Sachs
Steven M Seaver
Malvika A Shah
Naoko Shinozawa
Filippo Soave
Christopher J Stansfield
Robert J Tarbell
Raymond Texeira
Henry R Weinberg
Jennifer L Weiss
Peter B Wolcott-Schickler
Steven T Wong
Michael T Woodland
Nima Yadollahpour
Nora B Zaldivar
Jeffrey R Zynda
Dena R Zyroff

Past Principals

Fredrick Markus
Paul Nocka
David Rowan
Janet Baum
Henry Chao
John Dellea
Robert DeVries
Robert Grow
Peter Haney
Vance Hosford
Dennis Kaiser
Mozhan Khadem
Gary Lahey
Richard Martin
Daniel Meus
John Ruffing
Jonathan Warburg
William Wilson
Evans Woollen

Past Staff

Ghazal Abbasy
Christina Abel
Doran Abel
Jeffrey Abramson
Alfred Ahl
Onyekachi Akoma
Jody Alexander
Alexander Allam
Yvonne Allen Gleason
Manuel Alonso
Miguela Altiveros
Daniel Ambrose
Donna Anderson
Karen Anderson
Alexandre Andrade
Muzaffar Ansari
Ethan Anthony
Christiane Arnouts
Daniel Arons
Michael Aronstham
Paula Arruda
Ann Bach
Mary Baker
Christopher Bakkila
Marwan Bakri
Karen Balchunas
John Baldwin
Lauren Barbieri
Janice Barker
Thomas Barrie
Rania Bartick
Shannon Bassett
Kendall Bates
Martin Batt
Fredric Bautze

Heather Baxter
Rose Bayani
Marianne Beagan
Brendan Beazley
Antonia Bellalta-Osborne
Richard Benedict
Penelope Benith
Gizel Berkeley
Sarah Bernhard
Sumit Bhandari
Joel Bielawski
Christel Bivens
Marlon Blackwell
Lisa Blasioli
Michael Blier
Michael Blutt
Wendy Blutt
Karen Boardman
John Bogdanski
Christina Bolinger
Amal Boulos
Eileen Bouvier
Shantae Bowden
Elizabeth Bowen
Sally Bowman-Gordon
Ellen Brackett
Carlee Bradbury
Virginia Branch
Veronica Breckheimer
James Broady
Sean Brockette
Stuart Brodsky
Byron Bronston
Charles Brooks
Justin Brooks
Melanie Brooks
Amy Brown
Angela Brown
Thomas Brown
William Brown
Roger Brown
David Browne
Jennifer Buck
Cleary Buckley
William Bunting
Gerald Burger
Christine Bushey
Liesl Buskirk
Karen Button
Eileen Byrne
Marisol Caballero
Stephen Cabitt
Maria Cacciapouti
Cristina Campbell
Dianne Campbell
Barbara Cantwell
Anthony Cappoli

William Carpenter
Paul Carreiro
Mary Carter
Audrey Carty
Catherine Cassety
Valleri Castaldi
Daniel Castor
Michael Cavanaugh
Olivia Cejas
Rasa Cepas
Klaus Chalupa
Kimberly Chapman
Alfredo Chaves
Dorcas Chavez
Catherine Chen
Jocelyn Chen
Xiaohong Chen
Farzana H Chohan
Nancy Ciabotti
Deedee Ciancola
Johanna Ciccarelli
Martyn Clarke
James Cleary
Patricia Clooney
Michele Cloutier
Matthew Cohen
William Collett
Belinda Collins
Eleanor Collins
Matthew Collins
James Collins, Sr.
Geralyn Comeau
Paul Coneeny
Colleen Connor
Mark Connor
Cheryl Conover
Melanie Coo
Peter Cook
Nancy Cooper
Jane Cote
Nancy Coughlin
Alton Cox
Grace Cox
Collette Creppel
Allison Crosbie
Thomas Crowder
John Crowe
Daniel Crowley
Luis Curet
David Damon
Christine Dandeneau
Caroline Darbyshire
Gill David
Duncan Davidson
Tom Davies
Leonard Davis
Owen Davis
Eileen Day
Jose De Jesus
Pamela de Lalla
Rosario Del Rosario
Joseph Dellanno
Michael Dembowski
Laura Demurjian

David Demus
Karen Dendy
Amy Derbedrosian
Caroline Derbyshire
Robert Dermody
Victor DeSantis
Paul Desjardins
Antone Dias
Michael DiRamio
Daniel Discenza
Mason Disosway
Kelly Docter
Corinne Dolak
Maria Donahue
Kim Ddonnaruma
Tammy Donroe
Tomas Dordevic
Marina Dost
Robert Drake
Elizabeth Droescher
Gina Dubuisson
Christine DuFour
Chanda Dunbar
Melissa Easton-Sandquist
Michael Eastwood
Jessica Edwards
Wendy Edwards
Ronit Eisenbach
Suzanne Eklund
Petra Eldh
Leonel Elgio
Kenneth Ellis, Jr.
Campbell Ellsworth
Brandy Elser
Nancy Emmons
Susan Englert
Allison English
Judith Erickson
Meryl Ettinger
Gregory Ettridge
Mark Evans
Johanna Everett
Matthew Fabre
Reinerio Faife
Brad Fair
Edward Faldetta
Jennifer Farrington
Alexandro Feliciano
Julie Ferrari
Lisa Ferreira
Sybil Fickett-Jones
Darell Fields
Heather Fife
Amy Finch
Brian Finnigan
Adriana Finnvold
Dolores Fiore
MIchael Fiorillo
Dianne Fish
Claire Fitzmaurice
Lisa Flagg
Paul Flaherty
Jason Flint
Jennifer Foncannon

Christann Foote
Melanie Fournier
John Fowler
Livia Franca
Carolyn Friedman
Jonathan Friend
Kazumitsu Fujihashi
Bruce Fullerton
Richard Fullerton
Peter Funk
Mark Gabriel
Michael Gale
Peter Gallagher
Deveney Gallant
Kimberly Gardner
Jerzy Gardulski
Michael Garron
Mary Gaynor
Christine Gelhaus
Gerard Georges
Mark Gerwing
Denise Giarla
David Gill
Deborah Gladstone
Marcus Gleysteen
Leslie Glynn
Daniel Goddard
Aaron Goff
Stephanie Goldberg
Pamela Goldman
Nirmala Gonsalves
Norman Goulet
Birgit Graeve
Roger Grave de Peralta
Mary Graves
Spencer Gray
Susan Gray
Peter Greenberg
Steven Gribbin
Michael Griffin
Eugenia Grigoris
Thomas Grimble
Jo Grisham
William Grover
Dennis Grudkowski
Irwin Gueco
Nicholas Guerriero
Roberta Guerriero
Grace Guggenheim
Meagan Guillory
Nancy Hackett
Heather Hammatt
Li Hong Han
Dorothy Haney
Chuck Hannon
Dorrie Harllee
Susan Harrah
David Harris, Jr.
Michael Haskovec
Valerie Hayes
Lisa Hellmuth
Audrey Henderson
Christopher Henderson
Diane Henderson

Ronald Henderson
Sandra Henderson
Sara Hennessey
Matthew Herman
Yeida Hernandez
James Heroux
Lori Hessamfar
Olexa Hewryk
Michael Hinchcliffe
Jeffrey Hirsch
Jill Hitchen
Werner Hofmann
John Hollingsworth
Christina Holmes
Devon Holmes
Eric Holmquist
Pauline Holson
Emil Hoogendoorn
Deborah Hopper
Jeffrey Hoseth
Ellen Hughes
Jena Hwang
Myles Hyman
Christina Iacone
John Ihns
Janice Izenberg
Michael Jacobs
Todd Jacobsen
Beth Jacobson
Jeffrey Jacoby
Gina Jean
Brenda Jenkins
Gail Jewell
Constance Johson
David Johnson
Genae Johnson
Lorraine Johnson
Renee Johnson
Mary Lou Joseph
Annellen Joyce
William Kasdon
Anne Kearney
Lorraine Keating
Wayne Keenan
(Raburn) Monroe Kelly
Jonathan Kharfen
Kevin Killen
Juliann Kim
Jennifer King
Andrew Kiinoshta
Peter Kirkwood
Kristina Kitsopoulos
Kimberly Kloch
Dennis Kloko
Natalia Kogan
Hana Kolton-Patsouris
Neil Kosak
Beth Kostman
Ardys Kozbial
Alisa Kraus
Karen Krider
James Kukla
Mary Beth Kundrak
Brian LaBau

Margaret Lackner
Rodney Lamberson
Linda Lamoreaux
Christie-Lee Landry
James Langlois
Karl-Erik Larson
Nissa Larson
Lisa Laskos
Dana Laudani
Kelley Laue
Stacey Lavoie
Brenda Layne
Merritt Leavitt
Michael Leavitt
Eileen Leblanc
David Lee
Lorraine Lee
James Leslie
Richard Lesses
Preston Lightsey
Gregory Link
Nancy Linne
Carol Linscott
Shawn Liotti
Marcus Lisle
Andrew Liu
Elizabeth Losch
Susan Loughman
Dian Love
Linda Lukas
Denise Lyons
Elizabeth MacDonald
Chris Machold
Martha Macinnis
Charles MacKinnon
Pauline Magee
Christa Mahar
Blaze Makoid
Joanna Malenfant
Matthew Manke
Frances Manz
Christina Marchand
Jeanne Marchand
Timothy Marsters
John Martin
Neil Martin
Corinne Martinez
Jacinto Martinez
Jennifer Mason
Vicki Match-Suna
Charlotte Matthews
Gregory Matthews
Michelle Matz
James Maynard
Randy Mazin
Leslie McAdams
Heidi Mcallister
Albert McCarren
Catherine McCarthy
Timothy McCarthy
James McComas
Michael McGarry
Joan McGaw
Clifford McGillivray

Gwendolyn Mckenzie
Jeanann Mckenzie
Deborah McKinley
Andrea McKinney
Robert McMahan
Michael McPherson
Rocky Medina
Janice Melnick
Cooper Melton
Daniel Merritt
Jennifer Meus
Keith Millay
Deann Mills
Andrea Miltenberger
Matthew Mindrup
Alfred Mitchell
Jessica Modery-Micucci
Victoria Mohar
Bernard Moore
Karleen Moorhouse
Patricia Moriarty
Kathleen Morris
Linvelle Morton
Gloria Mudogo
Amir Mueller
Daniel Mullaley, Jr.
Alyssa Murock
Leo Murphy
Dianne Murray
Timothy Myers
Mary Nagata
Joseph Naughton, III
Elizabeth Navarro
Susan Nebelkopf
Geoffrey Nelson
Janice Neri
Mark Nielsen
Timothy Nistler
Michael Noel
Paul Norris
Gregg Novicoff
Jennifer Oakes
Stanley O'Blines
Christian O'Brien
Michele O'Brien
Errin O'Connell
Kathleen O'Connell
James Oglesby
William O'Leary
Roy Oliveira
Lauren Olivier
Joanne Olsen
Christina Oltmer
Patricia O'Neill
Alba Ordones
Jennifer Ortiz
Rafael Ortiz, Jr.
Daniel Osborne
Deepika Padam
Diana Parker
Mareen Parrott
Jennifer Payette
Monte Payette
Scott Payette

Shelly Payette
Naomi Pearson
Jill Peavey
Donald Pellerin
Karen Petersen
Keley Petersen
Jason Petrelli
David Pezzini
Lauri Phelps
Lisa Phinney
Janet Pickering
James Pierce
Monica Pine
Jessica Pineo
Khalil Pirani
Jorges Pires
Susan Ponte
Anne Poon
Mindi Poston
Alfredo Pou
Christian Powers
James Powers
Michael Price
Sharon Price
Damon Pride
John Pynchon
Kevin Quan
David Quenemoen
Charles Quinn
Leslie Quinn
Susan Quinn
Coimbatore Raghuram
Ali Rahim
Wilhelmina Rainey
Yvonne Ramos
Sarah Ranson
Thomas Ratekin
James Ray
Mark Reed
Ali Reza
Edison Ribeiro
Jonathan Rich
Jason Richardson
Laura Richardson
Lucy Riggs
Rebecca Riley
Luis Riobueno
Christine Rivera
Heidi Rivers
Darren Rizza
Nancy Rizzitano
Christopher Rodriguez
Ezequiel Rodriguez
David Rogers
Geoffrey Rogers
Jonathan Rollins
David Romero
Nancy Roper
Elizabeth Rose
Jonathan Rosenbloom
Betsy Ross
Laurie Rothwell
Charles Rotolo
Christopher Rountos

Shaun Rourke
Charles Roy
Katherine Rubinyi
Walter Ruccolo
Richard Rundell
Brenda Runyan
Andrew Russin
Joshua Safdie
Gregory Saldana
Carlos Salib
Alberto Salvatore
Amy Sanidas
Lilliam Santana-Barrera
Vincent Santaniello
Robert Sanville
Javorka Saracevic
Fitzwilliam Sargent
Lawrence Sass
Leslie Saunders
Maribeth Sawyer-Bicknell
Sara Sayner
Christopher Scales
Elaine Scales
William Scanlon
Deena Scaperotta
Cynthia Schell
Brian Schermer
Eric Scheuer
Timothy Schmidt
Eric Schuldenfrei
Phillip Schuler
Judith Scottland
Jacqueline Scott
Paul Seaman
Callou Seward
Chanda Seymour
Geoffrey Sharpe
Gerald Shaughnessy
Margaret Shldon
Kimberly Sheppard
Jeanice Sherman
Julie Sherman
Hilary Shields
Terry Shininger
Mark Sich
John Sih
Eric Silinsh
Claire Silva
Carolena Sim
Stephen Sim
Ethel Sison
Janet Slarskey
Jiri Slosar
Amy Smith
Jerry Smith
Karen Smith
Martin Smith
Sharon Snapp
Katie Snell
Joann Sobchuk
Guillermo Solares
Linda Somma
Jamie Soter
Hector Soto

Nadim Souki
Carole Soule
Henry Spiers
Kenneth Springer
Deborah Stanton
Steven Starkie
Margaret Staruk
Charles Steele
Erica Steenstra
Jennifer Steffek
Katherine Stefko
Jason Stenger
Erika Stern
Kathy Stern
Laura Stevens
Peggy Stewart
Victoria Stewart
Carole Stone
Gabrielle Stone
Brandon Stover
Pat Strangie
Diane Strazzullo
Damon Strub
Kristyn Strules
Youngjo Sul
Daina Sutton
Nancy Sweeney
Peter Tagiuri
Fatima Taheril
Shiva Tavaf-Rashti
Earl Taylor
Sheila Taylor
Mark Tedrow
John Ternullo
Kim Thomas
Jacquelyn Thompson
Mili Tomanic
Kyle Tornow
Carlos Torres
Cryssantti Torres
Mary Ellen Tracy
Jennifer Trost
Karin Turer
Patricia Turner
Shannon Tymkiw
Michael Tyrrell
Nnema Ugwuegbu
Hubert Vale
Alexander Van Praagh
Mark Vanderlyn
George Varga
Sondae Varga
Ericson Vencer
Kiki Venios
Katherine Venzke
Kathleen Vick
Linda Vigliante
Reetika Vijay
Camilo Villa
Frank Vitiello
Eric Vogel
John Vogel
Ludwig Vollers
Paula Vollers

Jeff Wagner
Joseph Wagner
Karen Wagner
Lora Wagner
Samuel Walker
Jennifer Walsh
Katherine Walsh
Thomas Walsh
James Wasley
Jonathan Wwters
Stephen Watt
Louise Webber
Lynn Weiler
Ellen Weinstock
Al Weisz
Nathalie Weller
Tammer Weller
Britony Wells
Dahven White
Cecil Whyte
James Wilkinson
James Willard
Darrell Williams
Eileen Williams
Stacey Williams
Holly Williams
Paul Willis, Jr.
John Wilson
Mark Wilson
Lisa Winer
Gary Wingo
Robert Winstead
Julia Wirick
Donna Wisnaskas
Amy Witzel
Herman Woerner
Mark Womble
Steven Wonkka
Whitney Wood
Kathryn Wright
Inna Yekelchik
David Yocum
Paul Yuen
Laura Zaganjori
Paul Zembsch
Joseph (Yossi) Zinger

SELECTED PROJECT HISTORY

1970 – 1979

Androscoggin Valley Hospital
80-Bed Hospital
Berlin, New Hampshire

Eastern Maine Medical Center
Bangor, Maine

Emerson Hospital
Ancillary Services
Concord, Massachusetts

Emerson Hospital
Cummings Doctors Office Buildings
Concord, Massachusetts

Emerson Hospital
ER / Dietary
Concord, Massachusetts

Jordan Hospital
Plymouth, Massachusetts

Joslin Diabetes Foundation
Patient/Inpatient Treatment Facility
Boston, Massachusetts

Leonard Morse Hospital
Replacement Hospital
Natick, Massachusetts

Martha's Vineyard Hospital
Oak Bluffs, Massachusetts

Mary Lane Hospital
Expansion/Conversion to Medical Offices
Ware, Massachusetts

Mayo Clinic
Orthopedic Area
Rochester, Minnesota

National Iranian Steel Corporation
Healthcare Delivery System Master Plan
Aryashahr, Iran

Salem Hospital
Salem, Massachusetts

1980 – 1989

The Aga Khan University
Karachi, Pakistan

Anna Jaques Hospital
Additions
Newburyport, Massachusetts

Armed Forces Institute of
Rehabilitative Medicine
Rawalpindi, Pakistan

Armed Forces Medical City
Debre Zeit, Ethiopia

Athens Regional Medical Center
Outpatient Surgery
Athens, Georgia

Back Bay Racquet Club
Boston, Massachusetts

Berkshire Medical Center
Addition
Pittsfield, Massachusetts

Beverly Hospital
Clinical Laboratory
Beverly, Massachusetts

Boston City Hospital
Facility Master Plan-Programming
Boston, Massachusetts

Clark University
Arthur M. Sackler Science Center
Worcester, Massachusetts

Concord Hospital
Replacement of 240 Beds & Ancillary
Services
Concord, New Hampshire

Cooley Dickinson Hospital
Facility Master Plan
Northampton, Massachusetts

The Country Club
Brookline, Massachusetts

Dartmouth College
Thayer School of Engineering
Hanover, New Hampshire

Dartmouth-Hitchcock Medical Center
Physical Development Master Plan
Hanover, New Hampshire

Eastern Maine Medical Center
Addition
Bangor, Maine

Framingham Union Hospital
Clinical Facilities
Framingham, Massachusetts

Harvard University
Sherman Fairchild Biochemistry Laboratory
Cambridge, Massachusetts

Hotel on the Nile
Luxor, Egypt

Houlton Regional Hospital
Houlton, Maine

The Jet Spray Corporation
Corporate Headquarters
Norwood, Massachusetts

Mayo Clinic
Mayo Building Lobby Renovation
Rochester, Minnesota

Massachusetts General Hospital
Wellman Research Building
Boston, Massachusetts

Mid Coast Hospital
Brunswick, Maine

Middlesex Memorial Hospital
Addition and Renovations
Middletown, Connecticut

Mt. Desert Island Hospital
Obstetrics and Intensive Care Unit
Bar Harbor, Maine

New England Baptist Hospital
Boston, Massachusetts

New England Deaconess Hospital
Boston, Massachusetts

The Pennsylvania State University
Chandlee Laboratory Renovation
University Park, Pennsylvania

Princeton University
Lewis Thomas Laboratory
Princeton, New Jersey

Princeton University
Frick Chemistry Laboratory
Princeton, New Jersey

St. Mary's General Hospital
Lewiston, Maine

St. Mary's Hospital
Intensive Care Unit and Patient Rooms
West Palm Beach, Florida

Tufts University
Health Science Campus
Master Plan
Boston, Massachusetts

United States Navy Medical Clinic
Replacement Emergency Center/
Outpatient Clinic
Midway Islands

University Hospital
Renovations
Boston, Massachusetts

University of Massachusetts Medical Center
Parking Structure
Worcester, Massachusetts

University of Pennsylvania
Clinical Research Building
Philadelphia, Pennsylvania

Winchester Hospital Family Medical Center
Wilmington, Massachusetts

Youville Hospital
Chronic Care Unit
Cambridge, Massachusetts

1990 – 1999

The Aga Khan University
Master Plan Update
Karachi, Pakistan

The Aga Khan University
Nursing School Expansion
Karachi, Pakistan

The Aga Khan University
Research and Community Health Services
Center
Karachi, Pakistan

Aravind Eye Hospital
Coimbatore, India

Blue Cross/Blue Shield
Outpatient Clinics
Boston, Massachusetts

Brigham & Women's Hospital
Multiple Projects
Boston, Massachusetts

Carnegie Mellon University
Roberts Engineering Hall
Pittsburgh, Pennsylvania

Case Western Reserve University
School of Medicine
Richard F. Celeste Biomedical
Research Building
Cleveland, Ohio

Children's Hospital
Parking Garage
Boston, Massachusetts

Children's Hospital
Main Lobby Renovation
Boston, Massachusetts

Children's Hospital
Multiple Projects
Boston, Massachusetts

Clark University
University Center
Worcester, Massachusetts

College of Wooster
Severance Chemistry Building
Wooster, Ohio

Cornell University Medical College
Lasdon Biomedical Research Center
New York, New York

Duke University Medical Center
Medical Sciences Research Building
Durham, North Carolina

Duke University
Levine Science Research Center
Durham, North Carolina

Endicott College
Student Housing Building
Beverly, Massachusetts

Fenway Community Health Center
Boston, Massachusetts

Franklin and Marshall College
Pfeiffer Hall Renovation
Lancaster, Pennsylvania

Good Samaritan Medical Center
Emergency Surgery
West Palm Beach, Florida

Gordon College
Lane Student Center
Wenham, Massachusetts

Gordon College
Barrington Center for the Arts
Wenham, Massachusetts

Gordon College
Tavilla Hall
Wenham, Massachusetts

Greenwich Hospital
Bendheim Cancer Center
Greenwich, Connecticut

Hahnemann University and Hospital
Parking Garage
Philadelphia, Pennsylvania

Harvard University
Maxwell Dworkin Laboratory
Cambridge, Massachusetts

Harvard School of Public Health
Francois-Xavier Bagnoud Building
Boston, Massachusetts

Harvard University
Link Building
Cambridge, Massachusetts

Henrietta D. Goodall Hospital
Ambulatory Surgical Unit
Sanford, Maine

Hospital of the University of Pennsylvania
Patient Tower
Philadelphia, Pennsylvania

The Jackson Laboratory
Genetic Research Building
Bar Harbor, Maine

The Johns Hopkins Hospital
Outpatient Center
Baltimore, Maryland

KOÇ University
Master Plan
Istanbul, Turkey

Llttleton Regional Hospital
Facilities Master Paln
Littleton, New Hampshire

Massachusetts General Hospital
Wang Ambulatory Care Building, Level 6
Boston, Massachusetts

Mayo Medical Laboratories
Clinical Laboratory
Wilmington, Massachusetts

Mercy Medical Center
Cancer Center, Pediatric Unit,
Inpatient Rehabilitation Unit
Rockville Centre, New York

Merck
Master Plan
Rahway, New Jersey

Mid Coast Hospital
Multiple Projects
Brunswick, Maine

Middlebury College
Bicentennial Hall
Middlebury, Vermont

Ministry of Health
Evaluation of Healthcare System in Kuwait
Al-Ahmadi Region, Kuwait

New England Medical Center
Oncology Clinic
Boston, Massachusetts

New York University Medical Center
Skirball Institute for Biomolecular Medicine
New York, New York

Nursing Sisters of the Sick Poor
New Convent
Rockville Center, New York

Princeton University
Schultz Laboratory
Princeton, New Jersey

Princeton University
Chemical Engineering Quadrangle
Princeton, New Jersey

Rutgers University and the Robert Wood
Johnson Medical School
Center for Advanced Biotechnology and
Medicine
Piscataway, New Jersey

Sarah Lawrence College
Science Center
Bronxville, New York

Saints Memorial Medical Center
Multiple Projects
Lowell, Massachusetts

Sungai Petani Private Hospital
Sungai Petani, Malaysia

Tulane University
Environmental Sciences Building
New Orleans, Louisiana

University of Indianapolis
Martin Hall and Lilly Hall Renovation
Indianapolis, Indiana

University of Maine
Geological Sciences Center
Orono, Maine

University of Maryland
Physics Building
Catonsville, Maryland

University of Maryland at Baltimore
School of Medicine
Howard Hall Renovations
Baltimore, Maryland

University of Maryland Baltimore County
Biological Sciences Building Renovation
Catonsville, Maryland

University of Miami School of Medicine
Sylvester Comprehensive Cancer Center
Miami, Florida

University of Pennsylvania
Institute for Advanced Science and
Technology, Phase I
Philadelphia, Pennsylvania

University of South Florida
Moffitt Cancer Center and Eye Institute
Tampa, Florida

Vanderbilt University
Chemistry Building
Science and Engineering Building
Renovations
Nashville, Tennessee

Veterans Affairs Medical Center
Ambulatory Care Unit
Bedford, Massachusetts

Veterans Affairs Medical Center
Ambulatory Care Addition
Providence, Rhode Island

Virginia Commonwealth University
School of Engineering
Richmond, Virginia

Washington and Lee University
Science Center
Lexington, Virginia

Waterbury Hospital
Day Surgery Unit
Waterbury, Connecticut

Obsolete Military Camps Made into
Living Communities
Town Master Planning
Brandenburg, Germany

Wellesley College
Davis Museum and Cultural Center
Wellesley, Massachusetts

The William W. Backus Hospital
Ambulatory Care Building
Norwich, Connecticut

Worcester Polytechnic Institute
George E. Fuller Laboratories
Worcester, Massachusetts

Wyeth Research *(formerly Wyeth-Ayerst
Laboratories/American Cyanamid/Lederle)*
Pearl River, New York

Yale University
350 Edwards Street
New Haven, Connecticut

Youth Build / Boston
Boston, Massachusetts

2000 – Beyond

The Aga Khan University
Sports and Rehabilitation Center
Karachi, Pakistan

The Aga Khan University
Ambulatory Care Building
Karachi, Pakistan

The Aga Khan University
Women's Residences
Karachi, Pakistan

The Aga Khan University
Cardiac Services Building
(Khimji Building for Cardiac Services)
Karachi, Pakistan

Amherst College
Geology Building and Natural History
Museum
Amherst, Massachusetts

Biogen, Inc
Bio 8, Biological Research Facility
Cambridge, Massachusetts

Brown University
Barus and Holley Addition and Renovation
Providence, Rhode Island

Cambridge Hospital
Renewal and Expansion as a Center for
Community Health
Cambridge, Massachusetts

Emory & Henry College
Academic Center
Emory, Virginia

Gordon College
Science Center
Wenham, Massachusetts

Harvard University Art Museums
Fogg Museum of Art
Renovations and Additions
Cambridge, Massachusetts

Holyoke Hospital
New Facilities
Holyoke, Massachusetts

Indiana University
Institute for Molecular and Cellular Biology
Bloomington, Indiana

Johns Hopkins University
Broadway Research Building
Baltimore, Maryland

Massachusetts General Hospital
Building 114 Charlestown Navy Yard,
Center for Aging and Neurodisorders
Boston, Massachusetts

Massachusetts Institute of Technology
Microphotonics Building
Cambridge, Massachusetts

New Hampshire Health and Human Services
Renovations
Concord, New Hampshire

New York Medical College
Medical Education Center and Basic
Sciences Building Improvements
Valhalla, New York

Oberlin College
Science Center
Oberlin, Ohio

Ohio Wesleyan University
Science Facility
Delaware, Ohio

Parkland Medical Center
Inpatient Pediatric Unit
Derry, New Hampshire

The Pennsylvania State University
Chemistry Research Building
University Park, Pennsylvania

The Pennsylvania State University
Life Sciences Building
University Park, Pennsylvania

Princeton University
Guyot Hall Addition and Alterations
Princeton, New Jersey

Rockefeller University
New Research Building
New York, New York

Schepens Eye Research Institute
(affiliated with Harvard School of Medicine)
Addition and Renovation
Boston, Massachusetts

Seoul National University
International Vaccine Institute
Seoul, Korea

Shakespeare & Company
Multiple Projects
Lenox, Massachusetts

Transkaryotic Therapies
Interior Fit-Out
Cambridge, Massachusetts

University of Alabama at Birmingham
Center for Human Genetics
Birmingham, Alabama

University of Illinois College of Medicine
Research Building
Chicago, Illinois

University of Iowa College of Medicine
Medical Education and Biomedical
Research Facility
Iowa City, Iowa

University of Maryland College Park
Chemistry and Teaching Building
College Park, Maryland

University of Maryland at Baltimore
School of Medicine
Health Sciences Facility Phase II
Baltimore, Maryland

University of Pittsburgh School of Medicine
Biomedical Sciences Tower III
Pittsburgh, Pennsylvania

University of Vermont
College of Medicine
Health Science Research Facility
Burlington, Vermont

Veterans Affairs Medical Center
Ambulatory Care Addition
Boston, Massachusetts

Washington and Lee University
Sorority Housing
Lexington, Virginia

West Virginia University
Life Sciences Building
Morgantown, West Virginia

Yale University School of Medicine
300 Cedar Street
New Haven, Connecticut

Yale University School of Medicine
Amistad Street Clinical Fit-out
New Haven, Connecticut

Yeshiva University
Albert Einstein College of Medicine
New York, New York

231

AWARDS

2003

AIA New England
Annual Awards for Excellence in Architecture
Award for Design
University of Iowa
Roy J. and Lucille A. Carver College of Medicine
Medical Education and
Biomedical Research Facility-Building A
(In association with Baldwin White Architects)
Iowa City, Iowa

Society for College and University Planning
Excellence in Planning Award
Oberlin College
Science Center
Oberlin, Ohio

2002

American Institute of Architects
Intern Development Program
Firm of the Year Award
Payette Associates

Boston Society of Architects
Honor Award
Brown University
Barus & Holley Addition and Renovation
Providence, Rhode Island

Boston Preservation Alliance
Preservation Achievement Award in the
Category of Significant Restoration or
Renovation Preserving Boston's
Architectural or Cultural Heritage
Massachusetts General Hospital
Building 114 Charlestown Navy Yard
Center for Aging and Neurodisorders
(In association with The Architectural Team Inc.)

2001

AIA, Rhode Island Chapter
Merit Award
Brown University
Barus & Holley Addition and Renovation
Providence, Rhode Island

AIA, Indianapolis Chapter
Award of Merit
University of Indianapolis
Life Sciences Building and Lilly Science Hall Renovation
Indianapolis, Indiana
(In association with Odle McGuire & Shook Corporation)

AIA, Indiana Chapter
Award of Honor
University of Indianapolis
Life Sciences Building and Lilly Science Hall Renovation
Indianapolis, Indiana
(In association with Odle McGuire & Shook Corporation)

2000

AIA New England
Honorable Mention
Middlebury College
Bicentennial Hall
Middlebury, Vermont

AIA New England
Honor Award
Tulane University
Environmental Sciences Building
New Orleans, Louisiana
(In association with Wilson Architects)

Research & Development Magazine
Lab of the Year
Middlebury College
Bicentennial Hall
Middlebury, Vermont

Boston Society of Architects
Honor Award
Veterans Affairs Medical Center
Ambulatory Care Addition
Providence, Rhode Island

AIA, Rhode Island Chapter
Honor Award
Veterans Affairs Medical Center
Ambulatory Care Addition
Providence, Rhode Island

Boston Society of Architects and
City of Boston
Harleston Parker Medal
Wellesley College
Davis Museum and Cultural Center
Wellesley, Massachusetts
(In association with Rafael Moneo)

1998

Boston Society of Architects
New England Healthcare Assembly
Healthcare Facilities Design Award
Children's Hospital Lobby
Boston, Massachusetts

1997

Boston Society of Architects
New England Healthcare Assembly
Healthcare Facilities Design Award
Harvard School of Public Health
Francois-Xavier Bagnoud Building
Boston, Massachusetts

Concrete Reinforcing Steel Institute (CRSI)
Design Award, Regional Winner
Carnegie Mellon University
Roberts Engineering Hall
Pittsburgh, Pennsylvania

1996

Research & Development Magazine
Lab of the Year
Duke University
Levine Science Research Center
Durham, North Carolina

Precast Concrete Institute
PCI Design Award
Duke University
Levine Science Research Center
Durham, North Carolina

Precast Concrete Institute
PCI Design Award
Duke University Medical Center
Medical Sciences Research Building
Durham, North Carolina

Health Facilities Management Magazine
VISTA Award
University Hospitals of Cleveland
Alfred and Norma Lerner Tower,
Samuel Mather Pavilion
Cleveland, Ohio

Boston Society of Architects
Honor Award
Yale University
350 Edwards Street
New Haven, Connecticut

1995

Progressive Architecture
Laboratory Award
Biogen
Bio 6
Cambridge, Massachusetts

Identity Magazine
Design Award
Children's Hospital
Elevator Lobby
Boston, Massachusetts

National Commercial Builders Council
Grand Award
Duke University
Levine Science Research Center
Durham, North Carolina

Boston Society of Architects
Arts in Architecture Collaboration Award
Duke University Medical Center
Medical Sciences Research Building
Durham, North Carolina

National Commercial Builders Council
Merit Award
Duke University Medical Center
Medical Sciences Research Building
Durham, North Carolina

Concrete Construction Committee Award
Hahnemann University
Parking Garage
Philadelphia, Pennsylvania

Interiors Magazine
Honorable Mention for Interior Design
University Hospitals of Cleveland
Cleveland, Ohio

Progressive Architecture
Laboratory Award
Vanderbilt University
New Chemistry Building and Renovations for Chemistry,
Physics, Engineering, and Library
Nashville, Tennessee

Progressive Architecture
Laboratory Award
Washington and Lee University
Science Center
Lexington, Virginia

Greenwich Arts Council
Triennial Design Award
Greenwich Hospital Cancer Center
Cancer Center
Greenwich, Connecticut

Boston Society of Architects
Honor Award
University Hospitals of Cleveland
Cleveland, Ohio

1993

Association of University Architects
Design Award
Rutgers University and the Robert Wood Johnson Medical
School Center for Advanced Biotechnology and Medicine
Piscataway, New Jersey

Boston Society of Architects
New England Healthcare Assembly
Healthcare Facilities Design Award
Honorable Mention
University of Miami School of Medicine Sylvester
Comprehensive Cancer Center
Miami, Florida

1991

Modern Healthcare
Honorable Mention
Armed Forces Institute of Rehabilitative Medicine
Rawalpindi, Pakistan

Boston Society of Architects
Award for Excellence in Architecture
Boston Exports Award
Cornell University Medical College
Lasdon Biomedical Research Center
New York, New York

1990

Modern Healthcare
American Institute of Architects
Citation for Healthcare Facilities Design
University of Miami School of Medicine
Sylvester Comprehensive Cancer Center
Miami, Florida

1989

Boston Society of Architects
Boston Export Award
The Aga Khan University
Nursing School
Karachi, Pakistan

World Biennale of Architecture V
INTERARCH 89
The Gold Medal Special Prize of the Mayor of
the Town of Lille, France
The Aga Khan University
Academic and Medical Campus Buildings
Karachi, Pakistan

World Biennale of Architecture V
INTERARCH 89
Athens Regional Medical Center
Athens, Gorgia

New England Regional Council of the AIA
Award for Excellence in Architecture
Youville Hospital
Chronic Care and Rehabilitation Hospital Addition
Cambridge, Massachusetts

1988

Build Massachusetts
Massachusetts General Hospital
Wellman Research Building
Boston, Massachusetts

New England Regional Council
of the AIA
Honorable Mention
The Country Club
Brookline, Massachusetts

1987

New England Regional Council
of the AIA
Award for Excellence in Architecture
The Aga Khan University
Academic and Medical Campus Buildings
Karachi, Pakistan

American Institute of Architects
Honor Award for Architecture
Princeton University
Lewis Thomas Laboratory
Princeton, New Jersey
(In association with Venturi, Rauch and
Scott Brown Architects)

1986
Pennsylvania Society of Architects
Honor Award
Princeton University
Lewis Thomas Laboratory
Princeton, New Jersey
(In association with Venturi, Rauch and
Scott Brown Architects)

AIA, Philadelphia Chapter
Design Award
Princeton University
Lewis Thomas Laboratory
Princeton, New Jersey
(In association with Venturi, Rauch and
Scott Brown Architects)

Modern Healthcare
American Institute of Architects
Honor Award
The Aga Khan University
Academic and Medical Campus Buildings
Karachi, Pakistan

1985
National Endowment of the Arts
Design Arts Programs
Honorable Mention
Cityscape Design
Saint Paul, Minnesota

American Institute of Steel Construction
Architectural Award of Excellence
Massachusetts General Hospital
Wellman Research Building
Boston, Massachusetts

Associated General Contractors of
Massachusetts
Build Massachusetts Award
Massachusetts General Hospital
Wellman Research Building
Boston, Massachusetts

1984
Interiors Magazine
Interiors Award in Medical and Healthcare
Mayo Clinic
Rochester, Minnesota

1983
Women in Design International
Competition
Award in Architectural Design
Eastern Maine Medical Center
Bangor, Maine

World Biennale of Architecture II
INTERARCH 83
Houlton Regional Hospital
Houlton, Maine

1982
Venice Biennale
Architectural Award
The Aga Khan University
Academic and Medical Campus Buildings
Karachi, Pakistan

1981
Boston Society of Architects
Boston Export Award
The Aga Khan University
Nursing School
Karachi, Pakistan

1980
New England Regional Council
of the AIA
Honor Award
Back Bay Raquet Club
Boston, Massachusetts

Boston Society of Architects
Award for Excellence in Architecture
Boston Exports Award
Salem Hospital
Salem, Massachusetts

1979
Boston Society of Architects
Award for Excellence in Architecture
Boston Exports Award
Jordan Hospital
Plymouth, Massachusetts

1978
Massachusetts Department of
Environmental Affairs
Environmental Business Award
Joslin Diabetes Foundation
Boston, Massachusetts

1977
New England Regional Council
of the AIA
Honor Award
Houlton Regional Hospital
Houlton, Maine

1976
New England Regional Council
of the AIA
Honor Award
Anna Jacques Hospital
Newburyport, Massachusetts

1970
New England Regional Council
of the AIA
Honor Award
Emerson Hospital
Concord, Massachusetts

ACKNOWLEDGMENTS

Work represented in this monograph is
the result of significant collaboration
with our clients, associated architects,
consulting engineers, contractors, and
construction managers. We thank all of
them for the efforts they have put forth
in the realization of the work included in
this monograph. While our collaborators
are too numerous to mention, there are
a few that have been particularly
important and are due special acknowl-
edgment. To our clients, Biogen,
Genetics Institute, Gordon College,
Harvard University, Johns Hopkins,
Princeton University, Shakespeare &
Co., University of Iowa, University of
Maryland, Yale University, and others
who have provided us numerous
opportunities to assist them in the
development of their facilities we
extend our deepest appreciation.

To Bob Venturi, Denise Scott Brown,
Rafael Moneo, and Renzo Piano who
have enriched our practice through our
collaborations with them. To BR+A,
Vanderweil Engineers, and Simpson
Gumpertz & Heger, whose extensive
collaborations over the years have
supported many of the projects included in this book.

We would like to thank the individuals in
our office who spearheaded the
monograph effort: John Wilson, Kevin
Sullivan, Leon Drachman, Todd Sloane,
Ray Texeira, Yun Kyung Chung, Enno
Fritsch, and many others. Lastly,
a special thank you to Michael Crosbie
who provided editorial guidance on this
monograph.

PHOTOGRAPHY CREDITS

John Abromowski/Brown University: 172 (4)

Tom Bernard: 114 (1); 115 (2); 116 (4); 117 (5,6)

Mark Careaga: 61 (15,17)

Jon Chase/Harvard News Office: 156 (1) © 2003 President and Fellows of Harvard College

Rion Rizzo/Creative Sources Photography, Atlanta: 75 (11,12)

Michael C. Dersin: 86 (8)

Dave Desroches: 122 (1); 126 (6); 212 (1); 217 (5,6)

Paul Ferrino: 20 (1,3); 30 (3); 32 (6,7); 40 (3); 41 (4,5); 46 (1); 47; 48 (2); 49 (3,4); 66 (1); 70 (1–5); 71; 72 (6,7); 73 (8); 74 (9,10); 77; 79 (4–6)

Dan Forer: 20 (2); 23 (6); 84 (2,3); 85 (5); 86 (6,7)

Santiago Garay: 104 (7); 105 (8)

Jeff Goldberg/Esto: 15 (6); 16 (2); 18 (1); 145; 146 (3); 147 (5); 148 (6,8); 149; 158 (1); 159 (2,3); 160 (4); 161; 162 (7); 163 (8); 172 (1); 174 (5); 175 (6,7); 176 (8); 179 (2,3); 180 (4,5); 181 (6,7); 182 (8–10); 183 (11,12); 184 (1); 185; 186 (2); 187 (3–5); 188 (6–8); 189 (9,10)

Bob Handelman: 15 (5); 144 (1,2); 146 (4)

Chris Hildreth/Duke University: 92 (1)

Jonathan Hillyer/Esto: 107; 108 (2,3); 109 (4); 150 (1); 151; 152 (2); 153 (3,4); 154 (5,6); 155 (7)

John Horner: 134 (3); 135 (5)

Timothy Hursley; 128 (1); 129 (2); 130 (3,4); 131 (5,6)

Warren Jagger: 21 (5); 123; 124 (2); 125 (3); 126 (6); 127 (7,8); 190 (1); 191 (2,3); 192 (4); 193 (5–7); 194 (8,9); 195 (10,11); 198 (1); 199; 201 (4,5)

Jonas A. Kahn: 17 (3); 148 (7)

Mark Karlsberg/Studio Eleven: 13 (3)

Peter Lewitt: 16 (1); 22 (2); 100 (1); 101 (2,3); 125 (4)

Mahlon Lovett: 64 (1)

Tim Lynch: 13 (2)

Bruce T. Martin: 133; 172 (2); 173; 177 (11)

Peter Mauss/Esto: 19 (5)

Gregory Murphey Studios: 67 (2); 68 (5)

Neoscape, Inc.: 206 (7); 207 (8); 209; 213; 214 (2); 215 (3); 216 (4); 219; 221 (3)

Payette Associates: 136 (1); 178 (1); 198 (2); 200 (3); 202 (1); 203 (2,3); 204 (4,5); 205 (6); 210 (2); 211 (3); 218 (1); 220 (2); 221 (4)

Thomas M. Payette: 60 (10); 61 (13, 16); 106 (1)

The Rockefeller University: 208 (1)

Steve Rosenthal: 12 (1); 34 (2); 35 (4,5); 36 (6); 37 (9,10)

Steve Schram: 103 (5)

Todd Sloane: 17 (5); 134 (2); 162 (5,6); 163 (9); 172 (3); 177 (9,10)

Ron Soloman: 82 (1); 83; 85 (4)

Ian Charles Stewart: 59 (8)

John B. Sullivan, Jr. Corp. of NH, Inc.: 22 (3)

Brian Vanden Brink: 14 (1,3); 17 (4); 88 (1); 89 (2,3); 90 (4,5); 91 (6,7); 94 (1); 95; 96 (2); 97 (3,4); 98 (5,6); 99 (7); 102 (4); 103 (6); 118 (1); 119; 120 (2–4); 121 (5): 132 (1); 170 (4)

Peter Vanderwarker: 135 (4); 168 (1); 169 (2,3); 170 (5); 171 (6,7)

Ayesha Vellani: 52 (1); 57 (4); 58 (5)

Paul Warchol: 15 (4); 18 (2); 19 (4); 53; 55 (2); 56 (3); 58 (6,7); 59 (9); 60 (11); 61 (12); 63; 67 (3); 68 (4); 69 (6,7); 76 (1); 78 (2,3)

Matt Wargo: 21 (4)

Nick Wheeler: 18 (3); 22 (1); 23 (4,5); 31 (4,5); 33 (9); 35 (3); 36 (7,8); 38 (1); 39; 41 (6) 42 (1); 43 (2,3); 44 (4); 45 (5–7)

Woodruff/Brown Photography: 110 (1); 111 (2); 112 (3); 113 (4); 164 (1); 165 (2,3); 166 (4); 167 (5,6)

Seung Hoon Yum: 137 (2,3); 138 (4,5); 139 (6,7); 140 (8); 141 (9,10)

George Zimberg: 28 (1); 29; 30 (2); 33 (8,10)

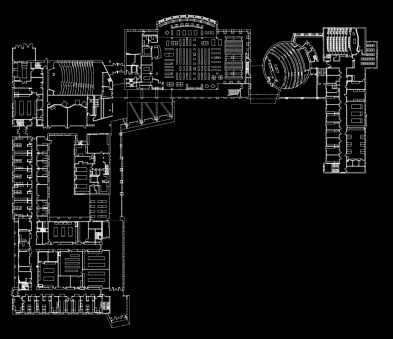

Oberlin College, New Science Center, OH

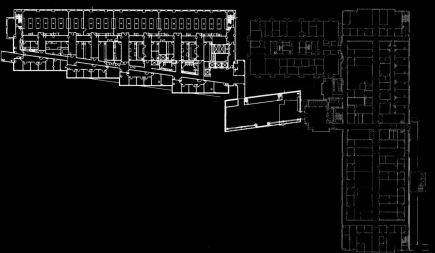

Johns Hopkins University, Broadway Research Building, MD

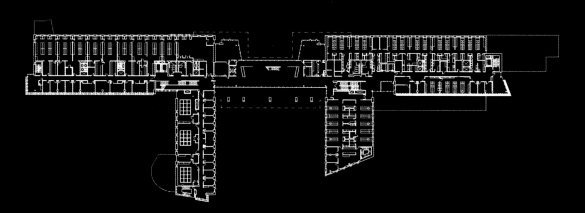

The Pennsylvania State University, Chemistry & Life Sciences Buildings, PA

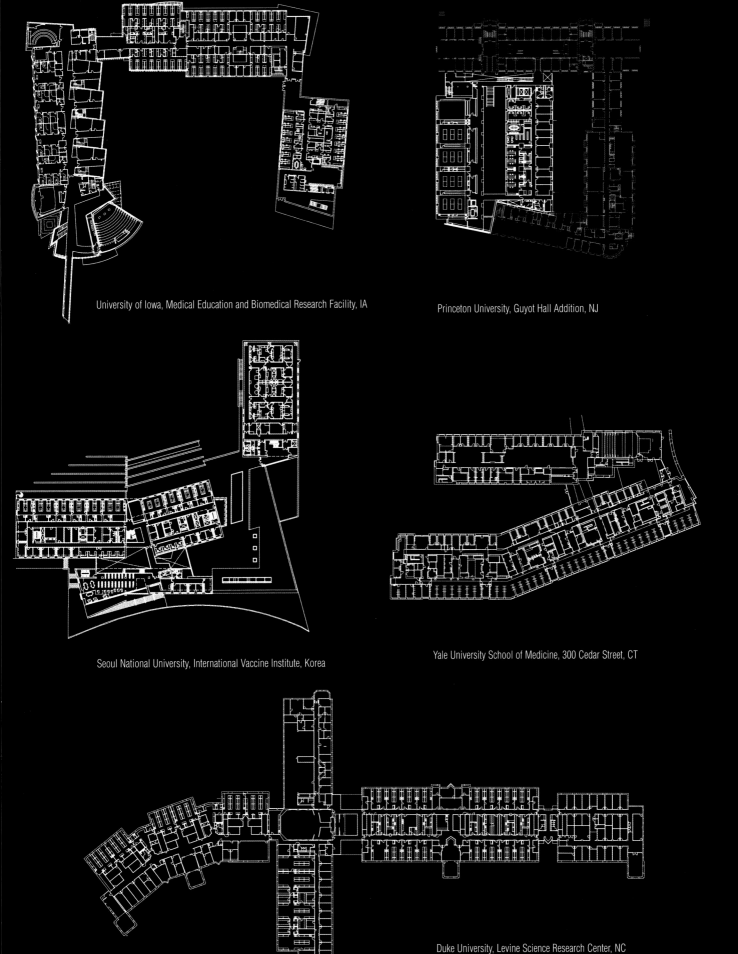

University of Iowa, Medical Education and Biomedical Research Facility, IA

Princeton University, Guyot Hall Addition, NJ

Seoul National University, International Vaccine Institute, Korea

Yale University School of Medicine, 300 Cedar Street, CT

Duke University, Levine Science Research Center, NC

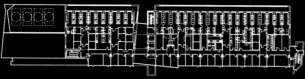

West Virginia University, Life Sciences Building, WV

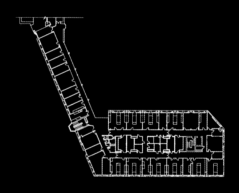

Washington and Lee University, Science Center, VA

Middlebury College, Bicentennial Hall, VT

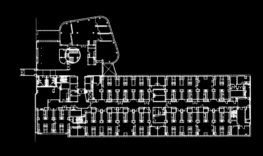

NYU, Skirball Institute for Biomolecular Medicine, NY

Duke University, Medical Sciences Research Building, NC

Harvard University, Sherman Fairchild Biochemistry Laboratory, MA

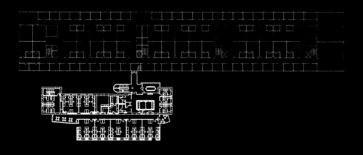

Tulane University, Environmental Sciences Building, LA

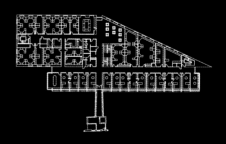

Harvard University, Maxwell Dworkin Laboratory, MA

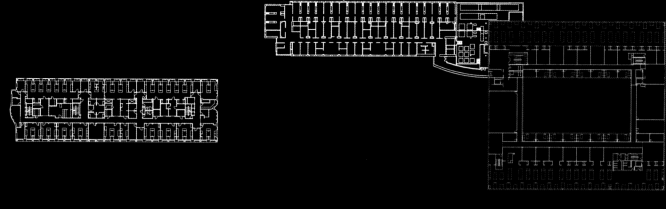

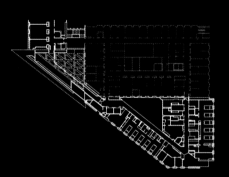

Princeton University, Lewis Thomas Laboratory, NJ

University of Vermont College of Medicine, Health Science Research Facility, VT

Massachusetts General Hospital, MA

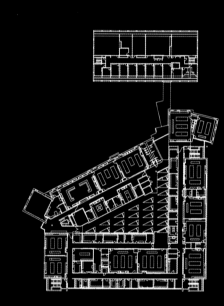

Ohio Wesleyan University, Science Facility, OH

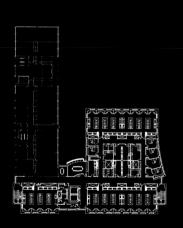

Harvard School of Public Health, Francois-Xavier Bagnoud Building, MA

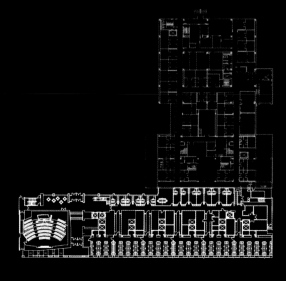

Vanderbilt University, New Chemistry Building, TN

University of Illinois at Chicago, Research Building, IL

Clark University, Arthur M Sackler Science Center, MA

Case Western Reserve University, Biomedical Research Building, OH

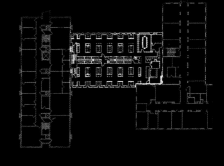

Harvard University, Link Building, MA

The Pennsylvania State University, Chandlee Hall Building, PA

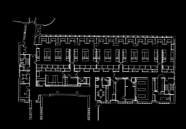

Princeton University, Frick Chemistry Building, NJ

Rutgers University, CABM, NJ

University of California at LA, Research Laboratories, CA

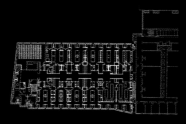

. UPENN, Institute for Advanced Science & Technology, PA

Carnegie Mellon University, Roberts Engineering Hall, PA

Rockefeller University, Research Building Renovation, NY

Wooster College, Severance Chemistry Addition, OH

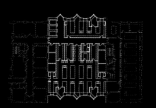

Cornell University, Lasdon Biomed Research Center, NY

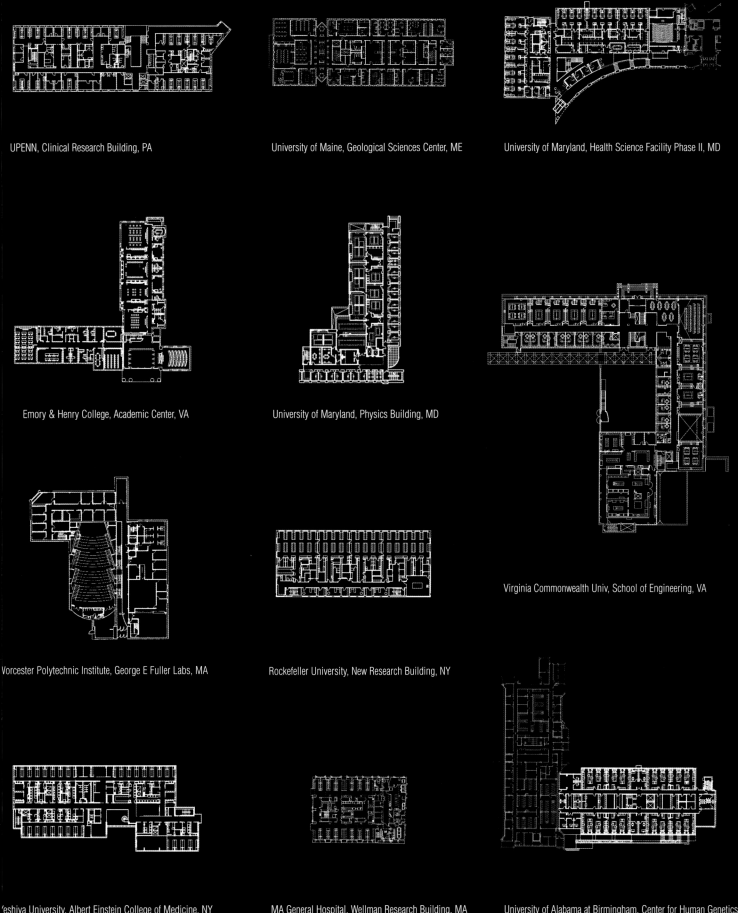

UPENN, Clinical Research Building, PA

University of Maine, Geological Sciences Center, ME

University of Maryland, Health Science Facility Phase II, MD

Emory & Henry College, Academic Center, VA

University of Maryland, Physics Building, MD

Virginia Commonwealth Univ, School of Engineering, VA

Worcester Polytechnic Institute, George E Fuller Labs, MA

Rockefeller University, New Research Building, NY

'eshiva University, Albert Einstein College of Medicine, NY

MA General Hospital, Wellman Research Building, MA

University of Alabama at Birmingham, Center for Human Genetics

Wyeth BioPharma, Building K, MA

The Jackson Laboratory, ME

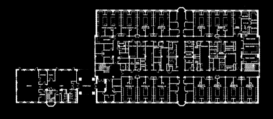

Wyeth Research, Lederle Laboratory, NY

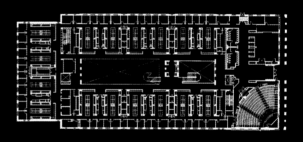

Wyeth Research, Chemistry Research Laboratory, NY

Biogen, Bio 6, MA

Biogen, Bio 9, MA

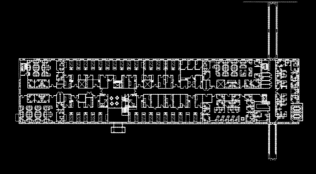

Wyeth BioPharma, Building F, MA

Wyeth Research, Building 200 Cambridge Park Drive, MA

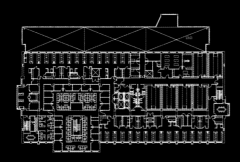

Wyeth BioPharma, Building G, MA

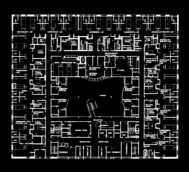

Wyeth BioPharma, MA

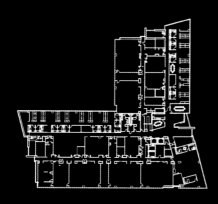

Biogen, Bio 8, MA

Schepens Eye Research Institute, MA

Mid Coast Hospital, ME

New England Baptist Hospital, MA

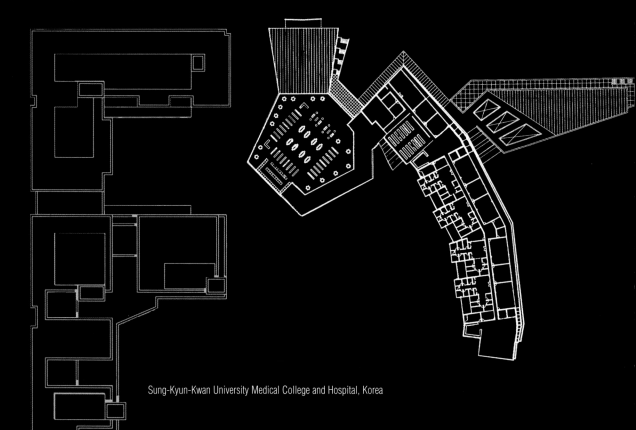

Sung-Kyun-Kwan University Medical College and Hospital, Korea

Houlton Regional Hospital, ME

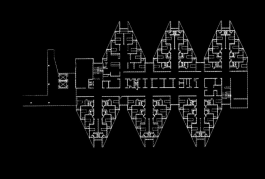

Jordan Hospital, MA

Leonard Morse Hospital, MA

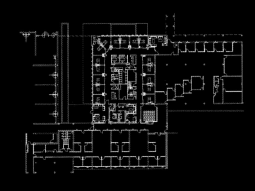

The Aga Khan University, Cardiac Services Building, CSB, Pakistan

Mid Coast Hospital, ME

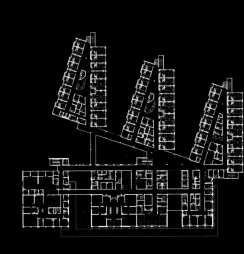

Sungai Petani Private Hospital, Malaysia

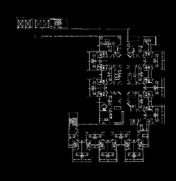

Anna Jaques Hospital, MA

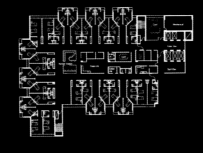

Eastern Maine Medical Center, ME

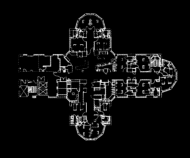

Massachusetts General Hospital, White Building, MA

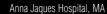

The Aga Khan University Hospital and Medical College, Pakistan

Emerson Hospital, ICU, MA

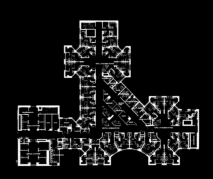

University Hospitals of Cleveland, OH

Androscoggin Valley Hospital, NH

New England Baptist Hospital, MA

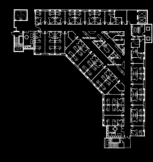

Kaiser Moanalua Medical Center, HI

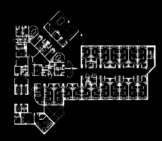

Youville Hospital and Rehabilitation Center, MA

Leonard Morse Hospital, ICU, MA

Leonard Morse Hospital, Inpatient Unit, MA

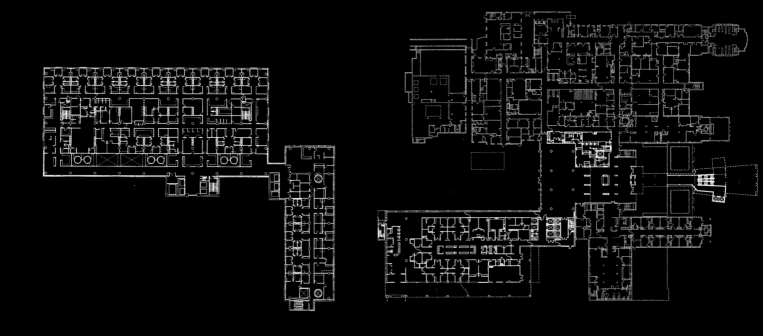

The Johns Hopkins Hospital, New Outpatient Center, MD

Good Samaritan Medical Center, FL

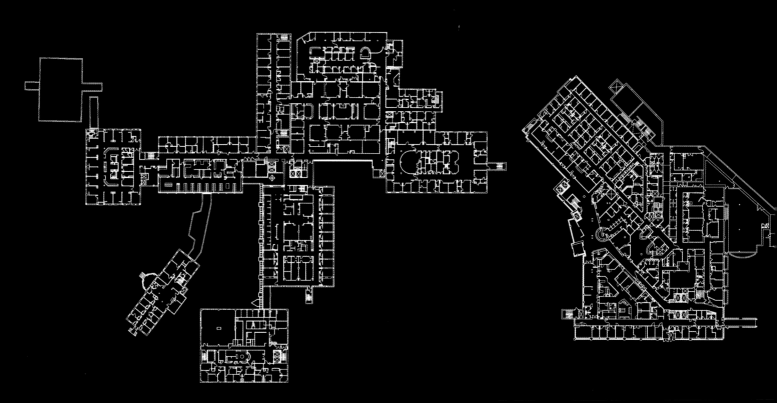

The William W. Backus Hospital, CT

Cambridge Hospital, MA

VA Providence, Ambulatory Care Addition and Renovation, RI

Greenwich Hospital, Cancer Center, CT

Athens Regional Medical Center, GA

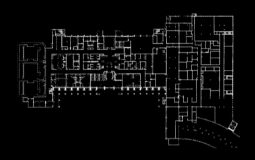

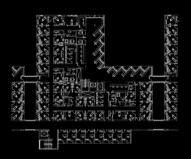

Mercy Medical Center, NY

University of Miami, Comprehensive Cancer Center, FL

The Aga Khan University, Ambulatory Care Building, Pakistan

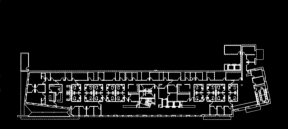

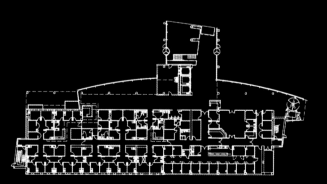

Yale University School of Medicine Ambulatory Care Building , CT

VA Boston, Ambulatory Care Addition, MA

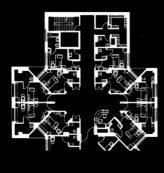

University Hospitals of Cleveland, OH

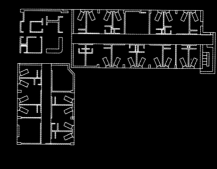

Houlton Regional Hospital, ME

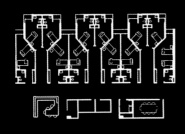

Eastern Maine Medical Center, ME

Jordan Hospital, MA

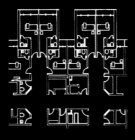

Anna Jacques Hospital, MA

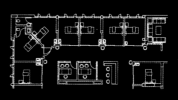

The Aga Khan University, Cardiac Services Building, Pakistan

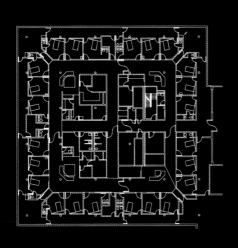

Athens Regional Medical Center, GA

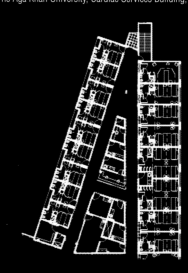

Sungai Petani Private Hospital, Malaysia

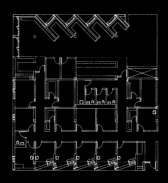

The Aga Khan University, Ambulatory Care Building, Pakistan

Yale University School of Medicine Ambulatory Care Building, CT

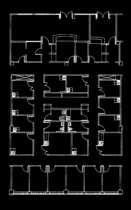

Cambridge Hospital, MA

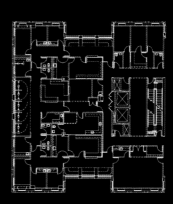

Greenwich Hospital, Cancer Center, CT

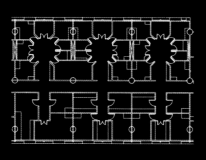

Johns Hopkins Hospital, MD

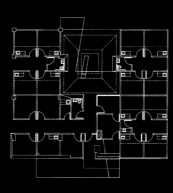

VA Providence, Ambulatory Care Addition and Renovation, RI

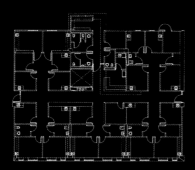

VA Boston, Ambulatory Care Addition, MA

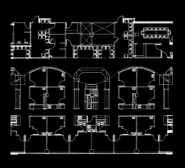

Massachusetts General Hospital, Wellman Research Building, MA